E S T A T E   P U B L I

C000144843

GLOUCESTER · CHEL

BISHOPS CLEEVE · QUEDGELEY · SHURDIN

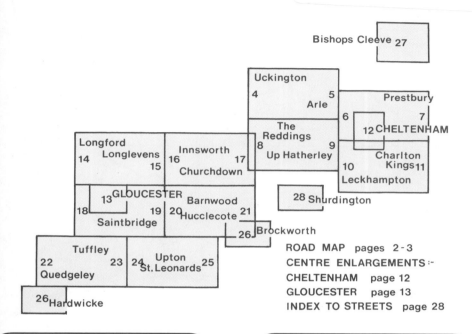

Bishops Cleeve 27

Uckington
4   5
Arle

Prestbury
6   7
12 CHELTENHAM

The
Reddings
8   9
Up Hatherley

Charlton
Kings 11
10
Leckhampton

Longford
14   Longlevens
15

Innsworth
16   17
Churchdown

13 GLOUCESTER
18   19 20 Barnwood
Saintbridge   Hucclecote 21

28 Shurdington

26 Brockworth

Tuffley
22   23 24 Upton
Quedgeley   St. Leonards 25

26 Hardwicke

Every effort has been made to verify the
accuracy of information in this book
but the publishers cannot accept
responsibility for expense or loss caused
by any error or omission. Information
that will be of assistance to the user of
the maps will be welcomed.

The representation of a road, track or
footpath on the maps in this atlas is no
evidence of the existence of a right of way.

One-way Street	→
Car Park	🄿
Place of Worship	✛
Post Office	●
Public Convenience	🄲
Pedestrianized	▨

Scale of street plans 4 inches to 1 mile
Unless otherwise stated

Street plans prepared and published by ESTATE PUBLICATIONS, Bridewell House,
TENTERDEN, KENT, and based upon the ORDNANCE SURVEY maps with the sanction
of the Controller of H. M. Stationery Office.

The Publishers acknowledge the co-operation of Gloucester City Council, Cheltenham B.C.,
Tewkesbury B.C., & Stroud D.C. in the preparation of these maps

Estate Publications 242 F   ISBN 0 86084 769 1   Crown Copyright reserved

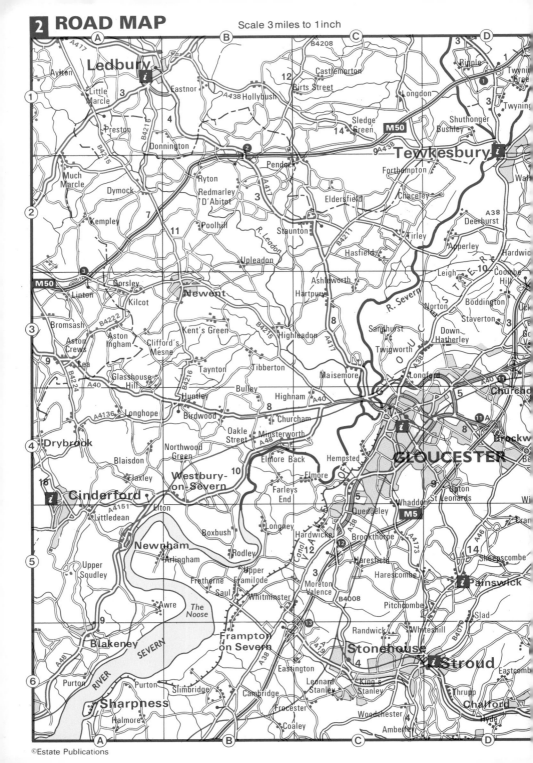

2 ROAD MAP

Scale 3 miles to 1 inch

©Estate Publications

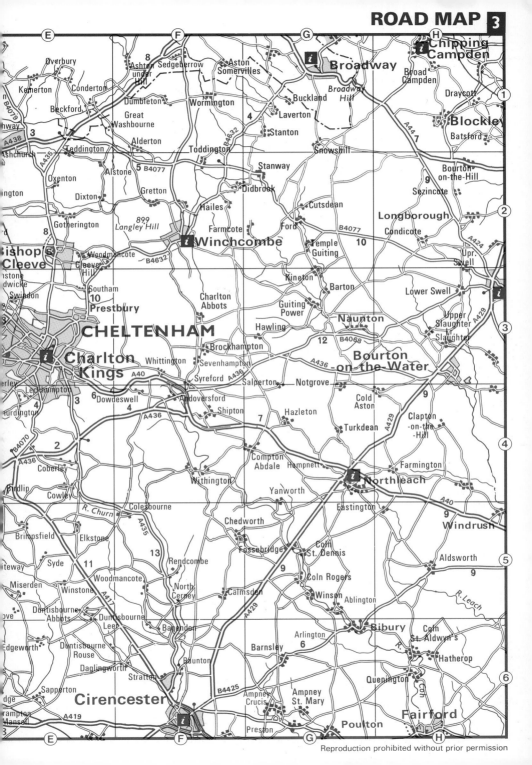

ROAD MAP **3**

Reproduction prohibited without prior permission

4 UCKINGTON

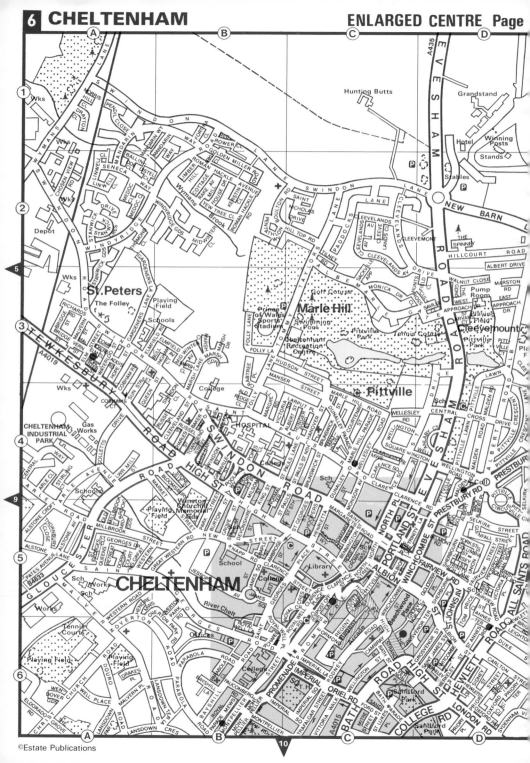

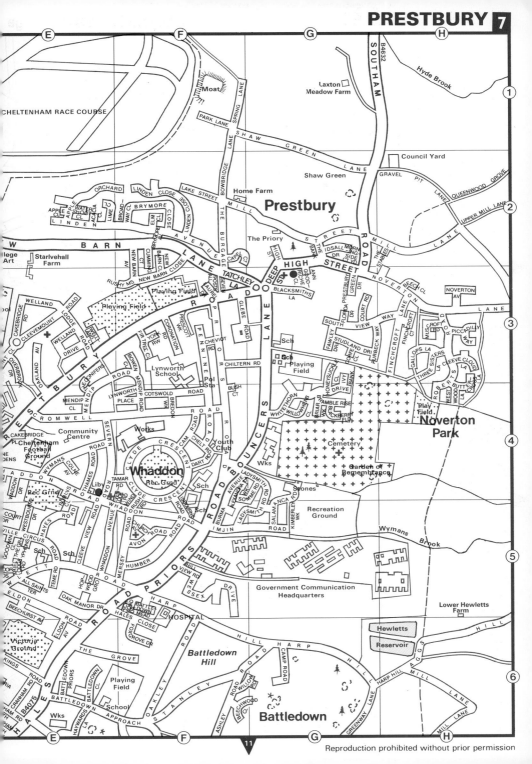

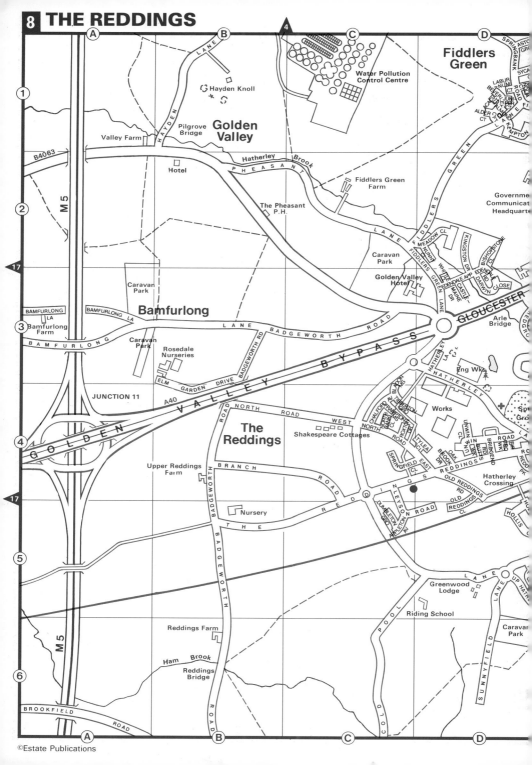

Fiddlers
Green

Water Pollution
Control Centre

Hayden Knoll

Pilgrove
Bridge

Golden
Valley

Valley Farm

Hatherley   Brook

Hotel

PHEASANT

Fiddlers Green
Farm

The Pheasant
P.H.

Governme
Communicat
Headquarte

Caravan
Park

Golden Valley
Hotel

Caravan
Park

Bamfurlong

GLOUCESTER

Arle
Bridge

BAMFURLONG

Bamfurlong
LA

BAMFURLONG LA

Bamfurlong
Farm

LANE   BADGEWORTH   ROAD

Eng Wks

HATHERLEY

Caravan
Park

Rosedale
Nurseries

ELM   GARDEN   DRIVE

Works

Sp
Gro

JUNCTION 11

A40

NORTH   ROAD

WEST

The
Reddings

Shakespeare Cottages

GOLDEN   VALLEY   BYPASS

Upper Reddings
Farm

BRANCH

Hatherley
Crossing

Nursery

Greenwood
Lodge

Reddings Farm

Riding School

Caravan
Park

Ham   Brook

Reddings
Bridge

BROOKFIELD   ROAD

M 5

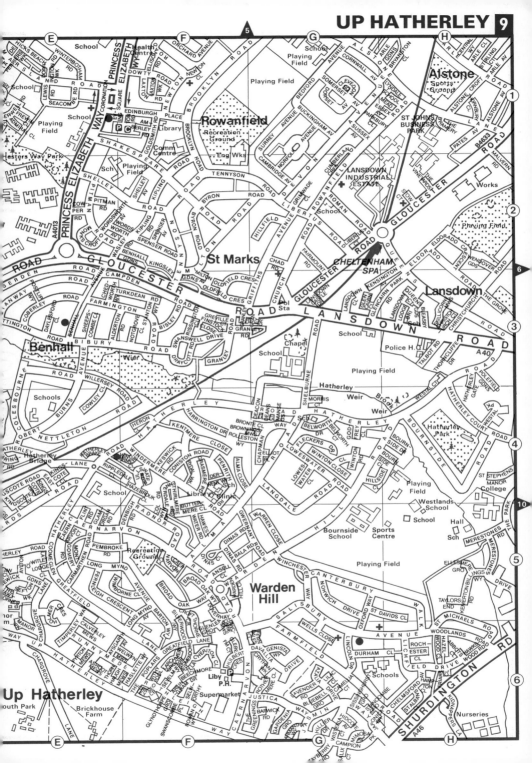

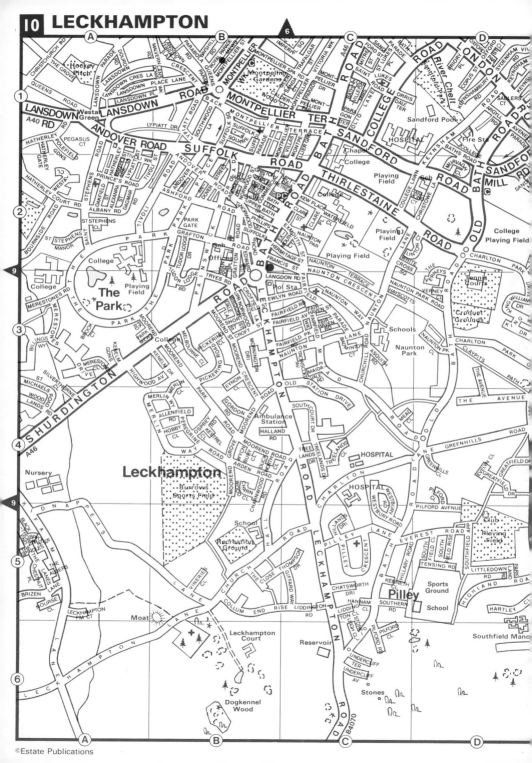

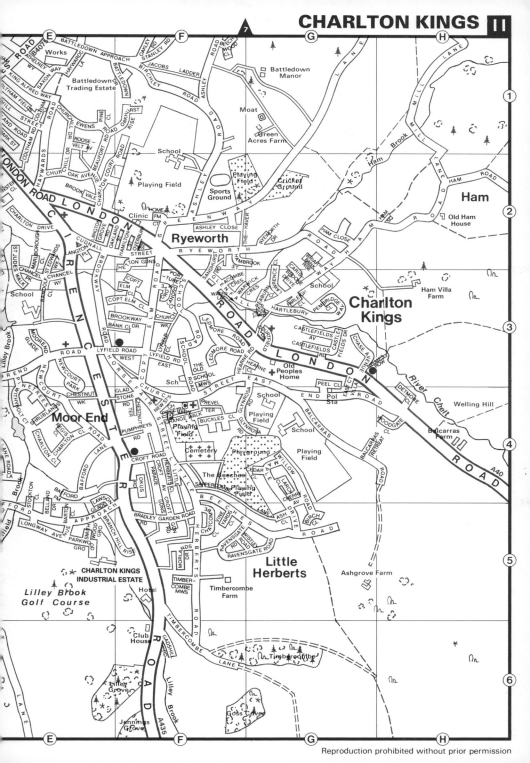

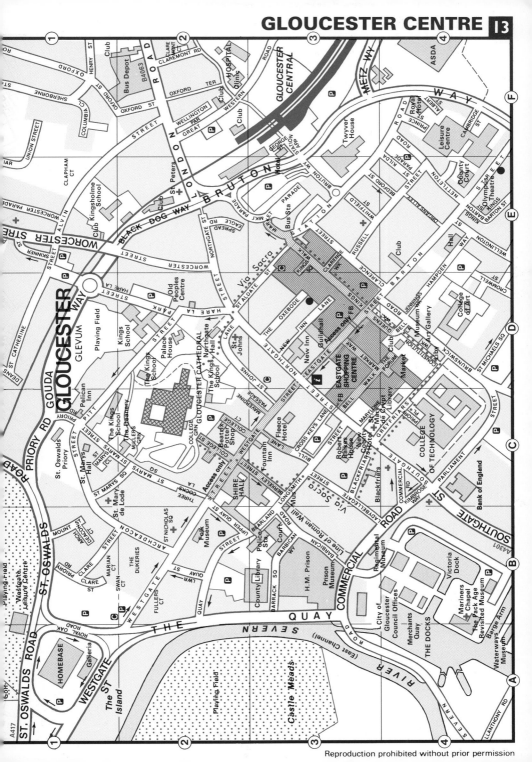

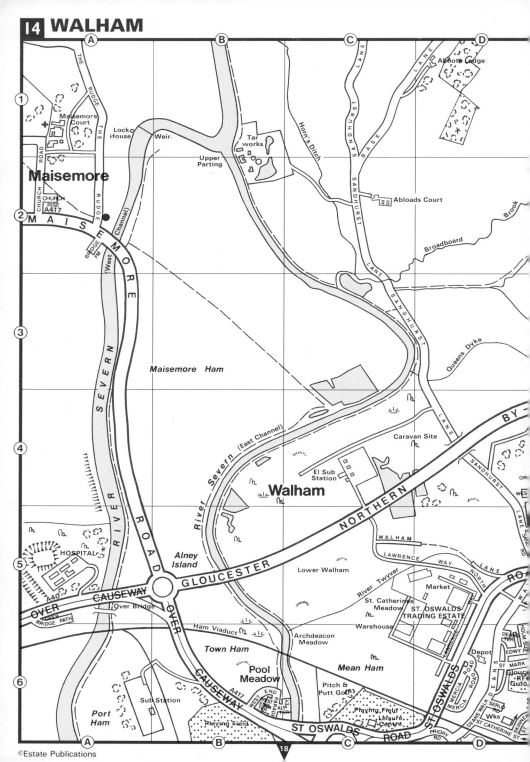

Maisemore Court

Lock House

Weir

Upper Parting

Tar works

Horn's Ditch

Abbots Lodge

Abloads Court

Broadboard

Brook

Maisemore

CHURCH ROAD
CHURCH RISE
A417

M A I S E M O R E

BRIDGE RM

(West Channel)

RUDGE

THE RUDGE

SANDHURST LANE

BASE LANE

SANDHURST LANE

Queens Dyke

Maisemore Ham

SEVERN

RIVER

ROAD

River Severn (East Channel)

Caravan Site

El Sub Station

Walham

NORTHERN

SANDHURST LANE

OR

WES

LANE SAN

RD

BY-

HOSPITAL

Alney Island

GLOUCESTER

CAUSEWAY

OVER

Over Bridge

OVER BRIDGE PATH

A40

WALHAM

LAWRENCE WAY

Lower Walham

River Twyver

St. Catherines Meadow

Market

ST. OSWALDS TRADING ESTATE

Warehouse

NORTH

LANE

RO

DEAN TER

EDWY R

Depot

Glouc
RF Grou

Ham Viaduct

Town Ham

Pool Meadow

A417

CAUSEWAY

Archdeacon Meadow

Mean Ham

Pitch & Putt Golf

Playing Field

Leisure Centre

ST OSWALDS

ROAD

MERCIA ROAD

DEANS WALK

ST CATHERINE ST

SERLO

SKINNER

PRIORY RD

Port Ham

Sub Station

Playing Field

WEST END PARADE

ST MARK

18

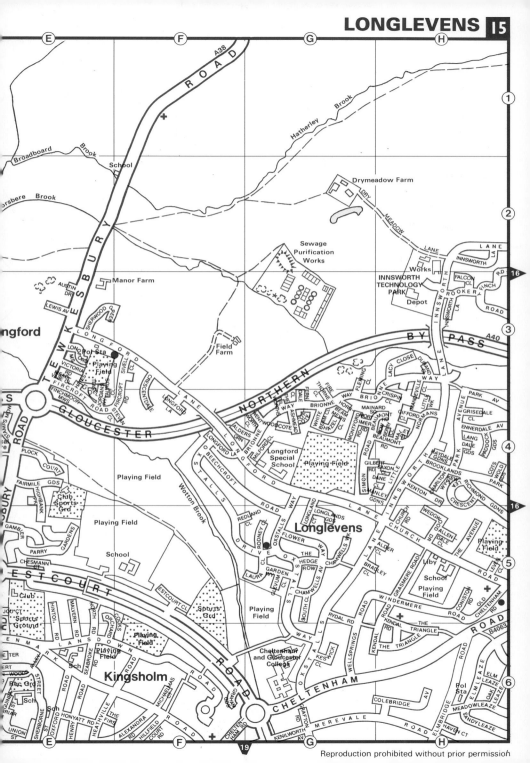

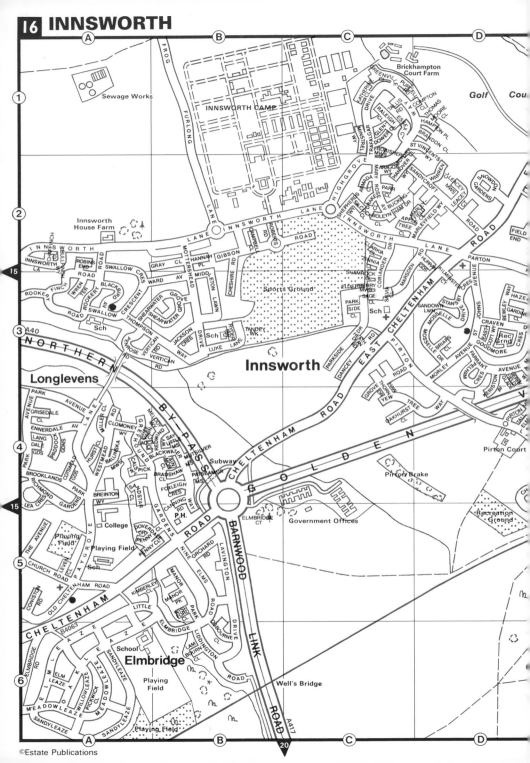

Sewage Works

INNSWORTH CAMP

Brickhampton Court Farm

Golf Cou

Innsworth House Farm

Longlevens

Innsworth

Sports Ground

INNSWORTH LANE

CHELTENHAM ROAD EAST

Subway

Government Offices

Pirton Brake

Pirton Court

Recreation Ground

Elmbridge

Playing Field

Well's Bridge

GOLDEN VALLEY

BARNWOOD LINK ROAD

NORTHERN BY-PASS

CHELTENHAM ROAD

GLOUCESTER & CHELTENHAM (STAVERTON) AIRPORT

CHELTENHAM ROAD
B4063 ROAD

BAMFURLONG
BAMFURLONG
Bamfurlong Farm
LA
LANE

M5
JUNCTION 11

BY PASS
A40

Parton Farm

SPRINGWELL GARDENS
WINSLOW
BUTTERMILK LANE

Evergreen Farm

Parton Manor

Norman's Brook

GOLDEN VALE
V.A.
QUINTON CL
GOLDEN

Home Farm

Community Centre

Churchdown

Playing Field

School

STATION ROAD
PARTON AVENUE
SUMMER LAND
Parton Court

M5

CROW BING
PARTON DR
HARRIS CL
AM S COCHRAN
SWORDFISH
SMITH CL
LEADER
BARNES WALK

STATION CL
STATION ROAD
STATION ROAD
Pol Sta
ALBERMARLE
CAVENDISH
TYNINGS CT
FAR SANDFIELD

Sports Ground

School

BROOKFIELD LANE

ANN HATHAWAY DR

ROAD

Playing Field

Sch

THE AVENUE
Liby
THE PIECE

SANDFIELD RD
KENT CL
KARBOURNE CRES
ORCHARD ROAD
BROOKFIELD ROAD

CORDINGLEY CL
CORDINGLEY LANE
BARNHAY
HOW CROFT
THE MANOR
CHURCH
BLACKSMITH LA
BROOKFIELD

Rec Grd
GREEN LANE
VICARAGE
CHAPEL
STATION ROAD
CHAPEL HAY LANE
CHAPEL HAY
DREWS
HAY
PAYNES PITCH
COURT
OLDBURY
ORCHARD
DUNSTANO
GLEN
CRANHAM LA
KINGSCOTE
CROFT CL
DIDBURY

Whitehouse Farm

Tinkers Hill

The Green

GREEN LANE
GRIFTYCRAFT LANE
BARROW HILL
HUCCLECOTE RD

BROCKWORTH ROAD

Churchdown Hill

Woodfield Farm

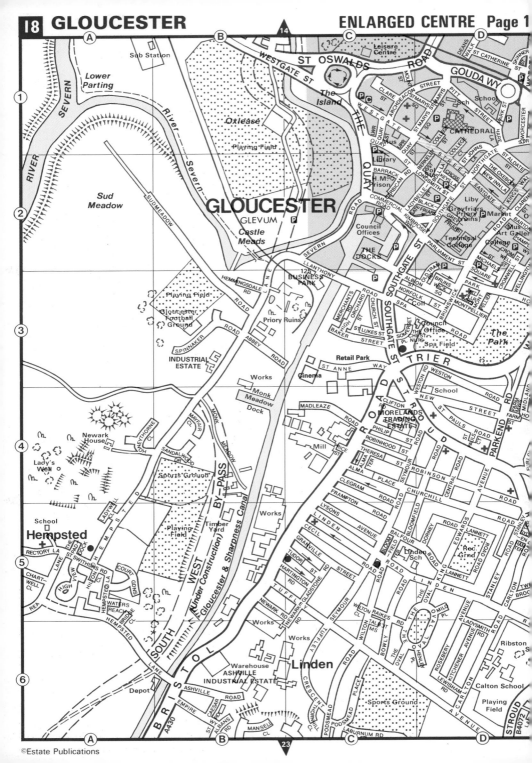

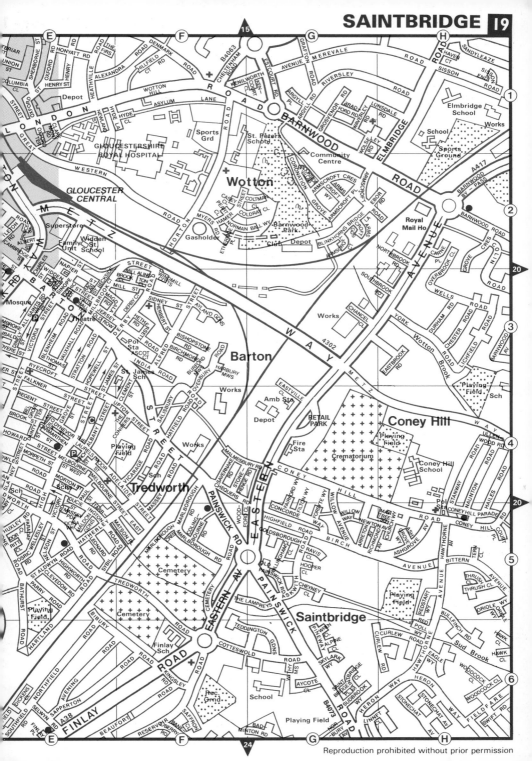

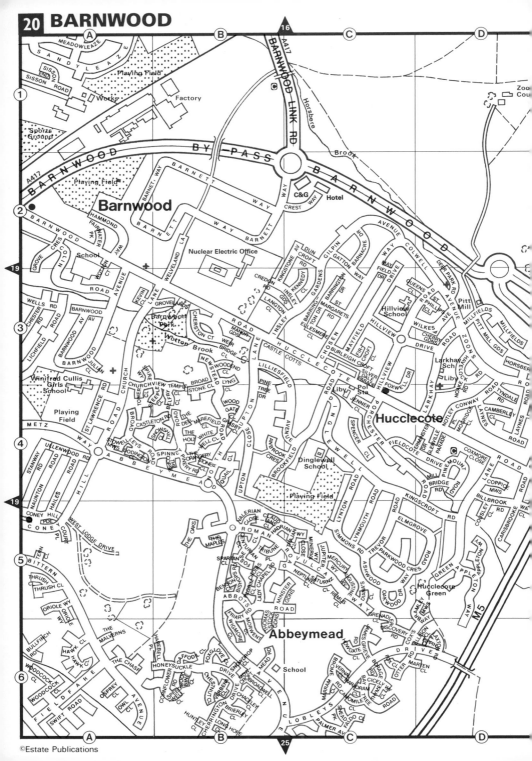

E   F   17   G   H

SOLDIERS WALK

Reservoir

The Brake

Reservoir

Churchdown Hill

The Coombs

Covered Reservoir

BROCKWORTH ROAD

Woodlands Farm

1

HUCCLECOTE LANE

LANE

M5

Pressmead Farm

2

Noake Court Farm

CHURCHDOWN

Dean Farm

3

an Villa (te of)

BROCKWORTH ROAD

4

BY PASS

SUSSEX GARDENS

SUSSEX GARDENS

COLERNE DRIVE

HUCCLECOTE

ROAD

CEDAR ROAD

MAPLE DR

Horsbere Brook

Brockwarth Court

Brockworth

MONTGOMERY CL

WEST END

FOLLAND

PRINCE JAMES

PRINCE ALBERT CT

ASTOR CL

WESTFIELD AV

ROWAN ROAD

ERMIN

GARDENS

ELM RD

OAK DRIVE

PARK DRIVE

PARK

CHASE

AVENUE

St ANNES

HICKLEY GDS

TANNERS

Playing Field

5

WESTFIELD

HILLVIEW AV

ERMIN

BOVERTON DRIVE

BOVERTON

St ANNES RD

FAIRHAVEN DR

ANSDELL

HURCOMBE WAY

MILL LANE

LANE

LANE

Mill Farm

Pol Sta

GOLF CLUB LA

BOVERTON

AVENUE

DRIVE

Liby

MOORFIELD

Sports Ground

Sch

CLYDE RD

TAMAR

TRENT ROAD

ERMIN

RIDGEMOUNT CL

VICARAGE COURT

SAYERS

MED WAY

LEADON CL

LEA ROAD

RD

6

GLOUCESTER TRADING ESTATE

I.C.I. Works

STREET

GREEN STREET

SEABROOK RD

GREEN BK

WAY

ABBOTSWOOD

DER WENT CL

CR

AIRFIELD

E   F   26   G   STREET A417   H

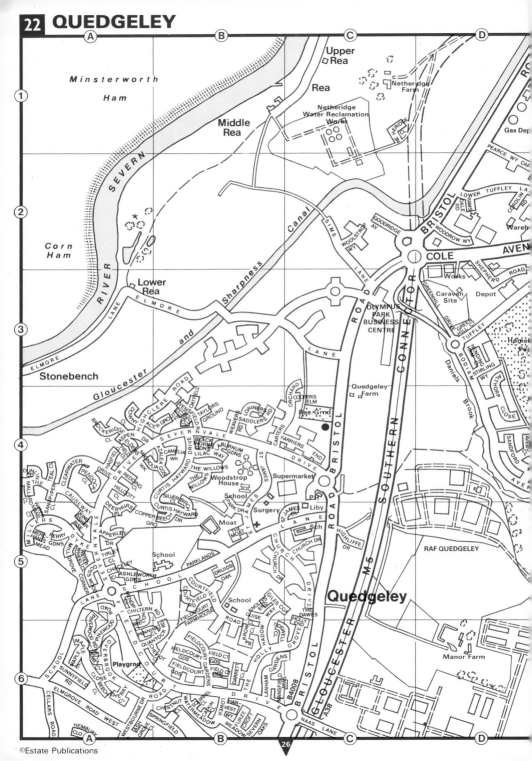

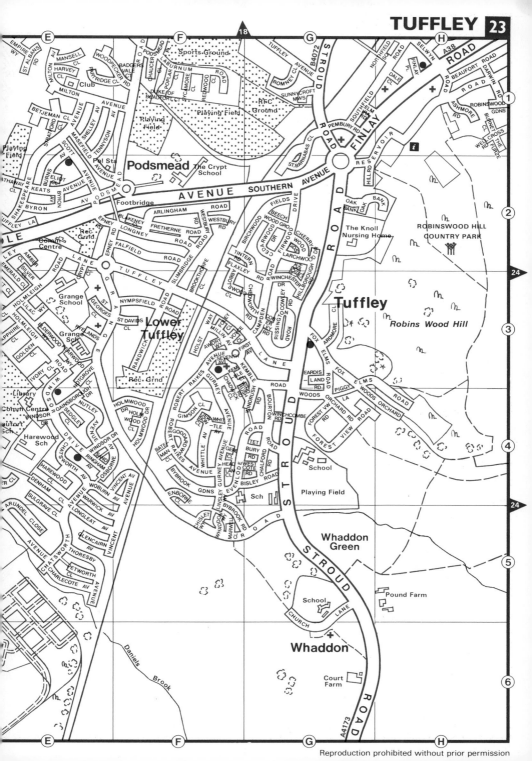

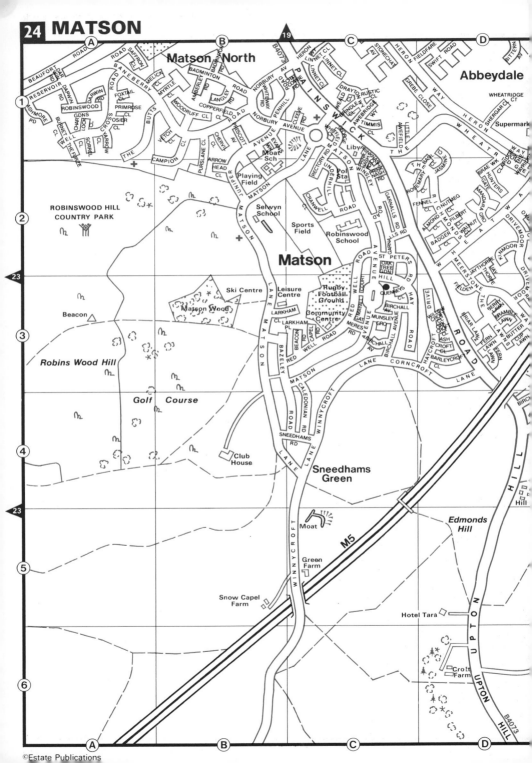

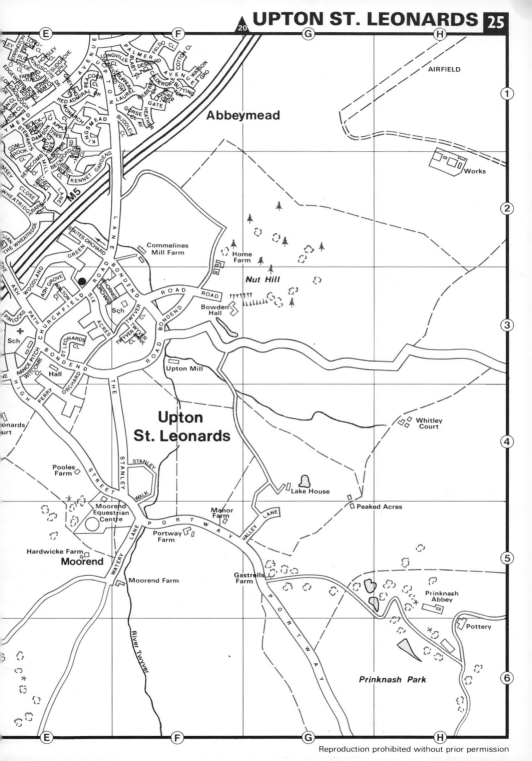

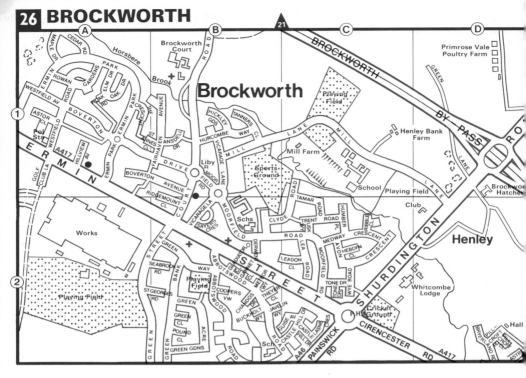

HARDWICKE

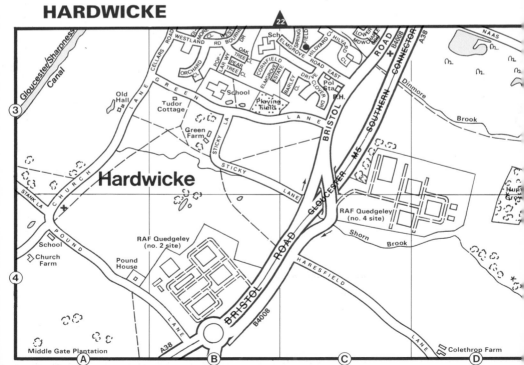

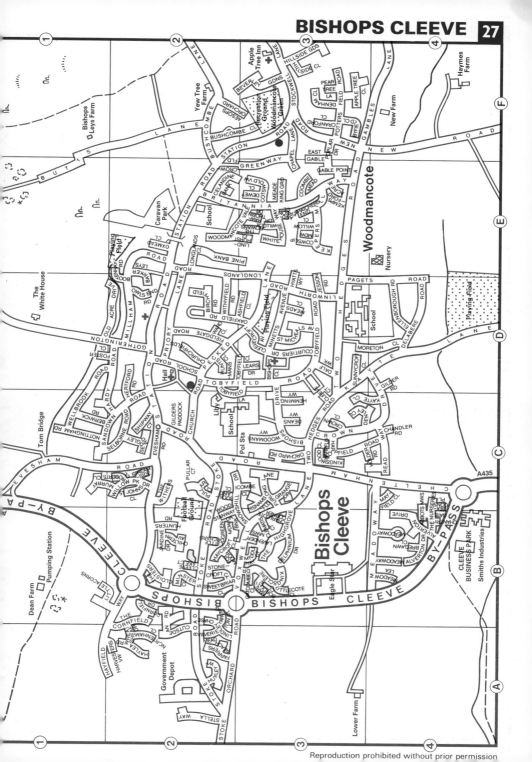

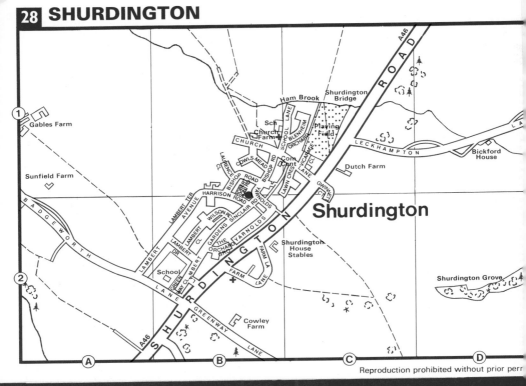

Gables Farm

Sunfield Farm

Ham Brook

Shurdington Bridge

Sch
Church Farm
Playing Field

CHURCH

COWLS MEAD

LAURENCE CL
BISHOP ROAD
BISHOPS RD

HARRISON ROAD

LAMBERT TER
LAMBERT AVENUE
LAMBERT CL
GARDENS
WILSON RD
SINCLAIR CL
THE ORCHARD
LAMBERT OR
GREEN WAY CL
LAMBERT

School

SHURDINGTON LANE

YARNOLDS
FARM LA
FARM LANE

SCHOOL LANE
BLENHEIM
ORCHARD
Com
LAWN CRESCENT
LANE
GWINN LA

LECKHAMPTON

Dutch Farm

Bickford House

Shurdington

Shurdington House Stables

Shurdington Grove

A46

BADGEWORTH

GREENWAY LANE

Cowley Farm

Reproduction prohibited without prior perm

A - Z INDEX TO STREETS
With Postcodes

The Index includes some names for which there is insufficient space on the maps. These names are preceded by an * and are followed by the nearest adjoining thoroughfare.

odmans Way. GL52 27 C3
odstanway Dri. GL52 27 B2
lington Clo. GL52 27 B2

CHELTENHAM

bots Clo. GL51 9 H6
acia Clo. GL52 7 E2
acia Ct. GL51 8 D1
omb Cres. GL52 11 F3
dis Rd. GL51 6 A3
miral Clo. GL51 9 E1
gs Hill. GL54 7 H6
any Rd. GL50 10 A2
emarle Gate. GL50 6 C3
ert Dri. GL52 6 D2
ert Pl. GL52 6 D5
ert Rd. GL52 6 D4
ert St. GL50 6 C4
ion Pl. GL52 12 D2
ion St. GL52 12 C2
ion Walk. GL50 12 C2
ershaw Clo. GL51 9 E5
erton Rd. GL51 9 E3
ridge Clo. GL50 6 B4
xandra St. GL50 10 A2
xandra La Walk. GL52 7 F4
Saints Rd. GL52 6 D5
Saints Ter. GL52 7 E5
Saints Villas Rd. GL52 6 D5
nfield Rd. GL53 10 B4
na Clo. GL51 9 F4
na Rd. GL51 9 F5
nond Ct. GL51 8 D1
tone Av. GL51 9 H1
tone Croft. GL51 9 H1
tone La. GL51 5 G6
berley Rd. GL51 9 F1
brose Pl. GL50 12 B2
brose St. GL50 12 A2
over Rd. GL50 10 A1
over St. GL50 10 B2
over Walk. GL50 10 B2
aby Ct. GL52 6 D4
e Goodriche Clo. GL52 7 G3
ell Clo. GL51 9 F5
le Clo. GL52 7 E2
le Orchard. GL52 7 E2
leton Av. GL51 8 C5
en Rd. GL53 10 B4
yll Rd. GL53 10 D1
l Lodge Rd. GL52 7 E5
e Clo. GL50 6 B2
Av. GL51 6 A4
Clo. GL51 6 A4
Dri. GL51 5 G6
Gdns. GL51 5 H6
Ind Est. GL51 5 H4
Rd. GL51 5 G5
ngham. GL51 9 F6
antha. GL51 9 G6
Clo. GL53 11 G5
cot Mews. GL51 9 E6
ford Rd. GL50 10 B2
ands Clo. GL51 5 E5
ands Rd. GL51 5 E5
ey Clo. GL52 11 F2
ley Rd. GL52 7 F6
uith Rd. GL53 10 C3
on Gro. GL51 8 D1
elney Way. GL52 11 E1
erstone Clo. GL51 4 D5
vood Clo. GL51 5 F4
nell Par. GL53 10 D1
n Rd. GL52 7 F5
on Clo. GL51 9 E5
garth Av. GL51 9 E6
ea Dri. GL51 9 G6

Albert Pl. GL52 6 D5
Montpellier Ter.
L50 12 A6
geworth Rd. GL51 8 B5
minton Ct. GL53 10 C3
ord App. GL53 11 E5
ord Farm. GL53 11 E4
ord Gro. GL53 11 E5
ord La. GL53 11 E4
house La. GL50 10 A2
r St. GL51 6 B4
Rd. GL51 9 F5

Balcarras Retreat. GL53 11 G4
Balcarras Road. GL53 11 G4
Ballinode Clo. GL50 6 A2
Bamfurlong La. GL51 8 A3
Bank Clo. GL53 11 E3
Bank Clo. GL51 5 E5
Barbridge Rd. GL51 5 F6
Barley Clo. GL51 5 E4
Barlow Rd. GL51 5 F5
Barnards Row. GL50 12 A2
Barnett Clo. GL51 5 E4
Barratts Mill La. GL53 12 D4
Barton Clo. GL53 11 E5
Barton Way. GL51 9 F5
Barwick Rd. GL51 9 G6
Bath Par. GL53 12 C5
Bath Rd. GL53 12 C6
Bath St. GL50 12 C4
Bath Ter. GL50 10 B2
Bathville Mws. GL53 12 C6
Battledown App. GL52 7 E6
Battledown Clo. GL52 7 E6
Battledown Dri. GL52 11 E1
Battledown Mead. GL52 7 F5
Battledown Priors. GL52 7 E6
Battledown Trading Est.
GL52 11 E1
Baynham Way. GL50 12 B2
Bayshill La. GL50 12 A4
Bayshill Rd. GL50 12 A5
Beale Rd. GL51 5 E6
Beale Walk. GL51 5 E6
Beaufort Rd. GL52 11 E2
Beaumont Dri. GL51 5 E5
Beaumont Rd. GL51 5 E5
Bedford Av. GL51 9 G1
Beech Clo,
Noverton Park. GL52 7 H3
Beech Clo,
Whaddon. GL52 7 E4
Beeches Rd. GL53 11 F4
Beechmore Dri. GL51 9 F6
Beechurst Av. GL52 7 E5
Beechwood Clo. GL52 7 F6
Belland Dri. GK53 11 E5
Belmont Rd. GL52 6 D5
Belmore Pl. GL53 12 C5
Belworth Ct. GL51 9 G4
Belworth Dri. GL51 9 G4
Benhall Av. GL52 9 E3
Benhall Gdns. GL51 9 F2
Bennington St. GL50 12 C2
Berkeley Pl. GL52 6 D6
Berkeley St. GL52 6 D6
Bethesda. GL50 10 B2
Beverley Croft. GL51 8 D1
Bibury Rd. GL51 9 E3
Billings Way. GL50 9 H5
Birch Clo. GL53 11 G5
Birchley Rd. GL52 11 F1
Bishopstone Clo. GL51 8 D2
Bisley Rd. GL51 9 F3
Blackberry Field. GL52 7 G4
Blacksmiths La. GL52 7 G3
Blackthorn End. GL53 10 A5
Bladon Mews. GL51 8 C4
Blake Croft. GL51 5 E4
Bleasby Gdns. GL51 9 H3
Blenheim Sq. GL51 5 F6
Bloomsbury St. GL50 6 B4
Bluebell Gro. GL51 9 G6
Bodnam Rd. GL51 5 F4
Boulton Rd. GL50 6 B2
Bouncers La. GL52 7 F4
Bournside Clo. GL51 9 H4
Bournside Dri. GL51 9 H4
Bournside Rd. GL51 9 H4
Bowbridge La. GL52 7 F2
Bowen Clo. GL52 7 F3
Bradley Rd. GL53 11 F5
Bramble Rise. GL52 7 G4
Bramley Rd. GL51 5 F5
Branch Hill Rise. GL53 11 E5
Branch Rd. GL51 8 B4
Brandon Pl. GL50 10 B2
Bredon Walk. GL52 7 F4
Brevel Ter. GL53 11 F4
Briar Walk. GL52 7 G4
Briarbank Rise. GL52 11 G2
Bridge St. GL51 6 A3
Bridgend Rd. GL51 8 D4
Brighton Rd. GL52 6 D6
Brizen La. GL53 10 A5

Broad Oak Way. GL51 9 F5
Broadway Clo. GL52 7 F2
Bronte Clo. GL51 9 F4
Brook Ct. GL50 10 A3
Brook Rd. GL51 5 H5
Brook Vale. GL52 11 E2
Brookfield Rd. GL3 8 A6
Brooklyn Clo. GL51 5 G5
Brooklyn Gdns. GL51 5 G5
Brooklyn Rd. GL51 9 F1
Brooksdale La. GL53 10 B3
Brookway Dri. GL53 11 F3
Brookway Rd. GL53 11 E2
Brown Clo. GL51 5 E5
Brownings Mews. GL51 9 F4
Brunswick St. GL50 6 C4
Bryaston Clo. GL51 5 H6
Brymore Av. GL52 7 F2
Brymore Clo. GL52 7 F2
Bryony Bank. GL53 10 A5
Buckingham Av. GL51 9 G1
Buckles Clo. GL53 11 F4
Bullingham Ct. GL51 6 B3
Burma Av. GL52 7 F5
Burton St. GL50 6 B5
Bush Ct. GL52 7 F4
Bushy Way. GL51 5 E4
Buttercross La. GL52 7 H4
Buttermere Clo. GL51 9 F5
Butts Walk. GL51 8 D4
Byron Rd. GL51 9 F2

Caernarvon Clo. GL51 9 F5
Caernarvon Ct. GL51 9 E5
Caernarvon Rd. GL51 9 E5
Cakebridge Pl. GL52 7 E4
Cakebridge Rd. GL52 7 E3
Calderwood Ct. GL50 12 B6
Calverley Mews. GL51 9 E6
Cam Rd. GL52 7 F4
Camberwell Rd. GL51 9 E1
Cambray Ct. GL50 12 C4
Cambray Pl. GL50 12 C4
Cambridge Av. GL51 9 G2
Camellia Ct. GL51 9 G6
Camp Rd. GL52 7 G6
Campden Rd. GL51 9 E3
Campion Park. GL51 9 G6
Canterbury Walk. GL51 9 G5
Capel Ct. GL52 7 F2
Carisbrook Dri. GL52 11 G3
Carlton Pl. GL51 6 B4
Carlton St. GL52 6 D6
Carlyle Gro. GL51 5 E4
Carmarthen Rd. GL51 9 E5
Carrol Gro. GL51 5 E5
Carter Rd. GL51 5 G4
Casino Pl. GL50 10 B2
Castlefields Av. GL52 11 G3
Castlefields Dri. GL52 11 G3
Castlefields Rd. GL52 11 G3
Castlemaine Dri. GL51 8 D3
Cedar Clo. GL53 11 G4
Cedar Court Rd. GL53 12 C6
Central Cross Dri. GL52 6 D4
Central Way. GL51 5 H6
Chad Rd. GL51 9 G2
Chalford Av. GL51 8 C4
Chancel Pk. GL53 11 E3
Chancel Way. GL53 11 E3
Chapel La. GL50 10 B2
Chapel St. GL50 12 A2
Chapel Walk. GL50 12 B4
Chapman Way. GL51 9 G4
Chargrove La. GL51 9 E5
Charles St. GL51 6 B4
Charlton Clo. GL53 11 E4
Charlton Ct Rd. GL52 11 E2
Charlton Dri. GL53 11 E2
Charlton Kings
Ind Est. GL53 11 E5
Charlton La. GL53 10 C4
Charlton Park Dri. GL53 10 D2
Charlton Park Gate.
GL53 10 D3
Charnwood Clo. GL53 10 B4
Charnwood Rd. GL53 10 B4
Chase Av. GL52 11 G3
Chaseley Cres. GL51 9 F6
Chatcombe Clo. GL53 11 F5
Chatsworth Dri. GL53 10 C5
Chedworth Way. GL51 9 E3
Chelmsford Av. GL51 9 H6

Chelsea Clo. GL53 11 E2
Chelt Rd. GL52 7 F4
Chelt Walk. GL51 5 G5
Cheltenham Trading Pk.
GL51 5 H6
Cheriton Clo. GL51 9 F6
Cherry Av. GL53 11 G4
Chester Walk. GL50 12 B2
Chestnut Pl. GL53 10 A5
Chestnut Ter. GL53 11 F4
Cheviot Rd. GL52 7 F3
Chestnut Walk. GL53 11 E4
Chiltern Rd. GL52 7 F3
Chosen View Rd. GL51 6 A2
Christchurch Ct. GL51 9 H3
Christchurch Rd. GL51 9 H3
Christowe La. GL53 10 D2
Church Av. GL52 7 F5
Church Piece. GL53 11 F4
Church Rd. GL53 10 B5
Church Rd. GL51 9 G3
Church Rd. GL51 5 H2
Church St. GL50 12 B2
Church St. GL53 11 F4
Church Walk. GL53 11 F3
Churchill Dri. GL52 11 E2
Churchill Rd. GL53 10 C3
Cirencester Rd. GL53 11 E2
Clare Pl. GL53 10 C2
Clare St. GL53 10 C2
Clarence Par. GL50 12 B3
Clarence Rd. GL52 12 D1
Clarence Sq. GL50 12 C1
Clarence St. GL50 12 B2
Clarington Mws. GL50 6 C4
Claypits Path. GL53 10 D3
Cleeve Cloud La. GL52 7 H3
Cleeve View Rd. GL52 7 E5
Cleeveland St. GL51 6 B4
Cleevelands Av. GL50 6 C2
Cleevelands Clo. GL50 6 C2
Cleevelands Dri. GL50 6 C2
Cleevemont. GL50 6 C2
Cleevemount Clo. GL52 7 E3
Cleevemount Rd. GL52 7 E3
Clevedon Sq. GL51 9 G1
Clyde Cres. GL52 7 F4
Coberley Rd. GL51 9 E3
Cobham Rd. GL51 6 A4
Cobhams Ct. GL51 6 A4
Cold Pool La. GL51 8 C6
Colesbourne Rd. GL51 9 E4
College Baths Rd. GL53 10 D1
College Lawn. GL53 10 C2
College Rd
Leckhampton. GL53 10 C1
College Rd, Cheltenham
Centre. GL53 12 C6
Colletts Dri. GL51 6 A4
Collum End Rise. GL53 10 B5
Colne Av. GL52 7 E4
Coltham Clo. GL52 11 E1
Coltham Fields. GL52 11 E1
Coltham Rd. GL52 11 E1
Columbia St. GL52 6 D5
Colwyn Dri. GL51 9 F5
Commercial St. GL50 10 B2
Compton Rd. GL51 6 A3
Coniston Rd. GL51 9 F4
Coombe Glen La. GL51 9 E5
Coppice Gate. GL51 5 F3
Copt Elm Clo. GL53 11 F3
Copt Elm Rd. GL53 11 F3
Copus St. GL53 10 D1
Corfe Clo. GL52 7 G3
Cornmeadow Dri. GL51 5 E4
Cornwall Av. GL51 9 G1
Coronation Rd. GL52 7 F3
Coronation Sq. GL51 9 E1
Cotswold Rd. GL52 7 F4
Cottage Rake Av. GL50 6 B2
County Court Rd. GL50 12 C3
Court Rd. GL52 7 G3
Courtenay St. GL50 6 C4
Courtfield Dri. GL52 11 G3
Cowley Clo. GL51 9 E4
Cowper Rd. GL51 9 E2
Crabtree Pl. GL50 6 B4
Cranham Rd. GL52 7 E6
Crescent Pl. GL50 12 B3
Crescent Ter. GL50 12 B3
Croft Avenue Par. GL53 11 F4
Croft Gdns. GL53 11 F4

Croft La. GL53 10 B3
Croft Par. GL53 11 F4
Croft Rd. GL53 11 F4
Croft St. GL53 10 B3
Croft Thorne Clo. GL51 9 F5
Cromwell Rd. GL52 7 E4
Crythan Walk. GL51 9 G6
Cudnall St. GL53 11 E2
Culross Clo. GL50 6 D3
Cumberland Cres. GL51 9 G2
Cumming Ct. GL52 7 F2

Dagmar Rd. GL50 10 A2
Dark La. GL51 5 H2
Dart Rd. GL52 7 F4
Darwin Clo. GL51 8 D3
Davallia Dri. GL51 9 G6
*David French Ct,
Farmfields Rd. GL51 9 G6
Daylesford Clo. GL51 9 E3
Deacon Clo. GL51 9 G4
Deakin Clo. GL51 5 H2
Deans Ct. GL51 9 G4
Deep St. GL52 7 G3
Deferriers Walk. GL51 5 E6
Denbigh Rd. GL51 9 F5
Derwent Way. GL51 9 F4
Detmore Clo. GL53 11 H4
Devon Av. GL51 9 G2
Devonshire St. GL50 12 A1
Dill Av. GL51 5 F5
Dinas Clo. GL51 9 F5
Dinas Rd. GL51 9 F5
Distel Clo. GL50 6 A2
Dog Bark La. GL51 5 F1
Dormer Rd. GL51 5 G5
Dorrincourt Mws. GL50 6 A5
Dorrington Walk. GL51 5 E6
Dorset Av. GL51 9 G1
Douro Rd. GL50 6 A6
Doverhay. GL51 9 F5
Dowty Rd. GL51 9 F1
Drakes Pl. GL50 6 A6
Draycott Rd. GL51 9 F3
Drayton Clo. GL50 6 A1
Duckworth Clo. GL53 10 B4
Duke St. GL52 6 D6
Dumbleton Gro. GL51 8 C5
Dunalley Par. GL50 6 C4
Dunalley St. GL50 12 C1
Dunbar Clo. GL51 4 D5
Dunster Clo. GL51 5 E6
Dunster Gdns. GL51 5 E6
Dunster Gro. GL51 4 D6
Dunster Rd. GL51 4 D6
Durham Clo. GL51 9 G6

East Approach Dri. GL52 6 D3
East Court Villa. GL52 11 G3
East End Rd. GL53 11 G3
Eaton Pl. GL53 12 C5
Edendale App. GL51 8 D3
Edendale Rd. GL51 8 D3
Edinburgh Pl. GL51 9 F1
Edward St. GL50 10 B2
Eldon Av. GL52 7 E6
Eldon Rd. GL52 7 E5
Eldorado Cres. GL50 9 H2
Eldorado Rd. GL50 9 H2
Ellesmere Gro. GL50 9 H5
Elliot Pl. GL51 9 G4
Ellison Rd. GL51 5 F6
Elm Clo. GL52 7 F2
Elm Clo. GL51 6 A3
Elm Garden Dri. GL51 8 B3
Elm St. GL51 6 A3
Elmfield Av. GL51 6 B3
Elmfield Rd. GL51 6 A3
Emperor Clo. GL51 9 E1
Ennerdale Rd. GL51 9 F4
Enterprize Way. GL51 5 H6
Essex Av. GL51 9 H1
Ettington Clo. GL51 4 D6
Evelyn Clo. GL53 10 D4
Evenlode Rd. GL52 7 E4
Everest Rd. GL53 10 C5
Evesham Rd. GL52 6 D1
Evington Rd. GL51 9 F1
Ewens Rd. GL52 11 E1
Ewlyn Rd. GL53 10 B3
Exmouth Ct. GL53 10 C2
Exmouth St. GL53 10 C2

Eynon Clo. GL53 10 B3
Fairfield Av. GL53 10 B3
Fairfield Par. GL53 10 C3
Fairfield Park Rd. GL53 10 B3
Fairfield Rd. GL53 10 B3
Fairfield St. GL53 10 B3
Fairfield Walk. GL53 10 C3
Fairhaven Rd. GL53 10 C3
Fairhaven St. GL53 10 C3
Fairmount Rd. GL51 9 G2
Fairview Clo. GL52 6 D5
Fairview Rd. GL52 12 D2
Fairview St. GL51 6 D5
Falkland Pl. GL51 5 E6
Faringdon Rd. GL51 9 E4
Farleigh Clo. GL52 11 G3
Farm Clo. GL51 5 E6
Farm La. GL53 10 A5
Farmfield Rd. GL51 9 G6
Farmington Rd. GL51 9 E3
Fauconberg Rd. GL50 12 A4
Fawley Dri. GL52 7 G3
Ferndales Clo. GL51 9 G6
Fernleigh Cres. GL51 9 E5
Fiddlers Green La. GL51 8 C2
Finchcroft Ct. GL52 7 H3
Finchcroft La. GL52 7 H3
Finstock Clo. GL51 9 F3
Fir Grove Walk. GL51 8 D4
Fir Tree Clo. GL52 7 F3
Fisher Walk. GL51 5 G4
Fleckers Dri. GL51 9 G4
Flint Rd. GL51 9 E5
Florida Dri. GL51 7 G3
Folly La. GL50 6 B3
Fortina Clo. GL50 6 B1
Foxgrove Dri. GL52 7 F6
Frampton Mews. GL51 8 C4
Francis St. GL53 10 B2
Frank Brookes Rd. GL51 5 G4
Frewin Clo. GL51 9 E1
Friars Clo. GL51 9 H6
*Fulbrook Clo,
  Pilgrove Way. GL51 5 E4

Gadshill Rd. GL53 11 F6
Gallops La. GL52 7 H3
Garden Rd. GL53 11 F5
Gardeners La. GL50 6 A3
Gardenia Gro. GL51 9 G6
Genista Way. GL51 9 G6
George Readings Way.
  GL51 5 G5
Giffard Way. GL53 10 C5
Gladstone Rd. GL53 11 F4
Glamorgan Rd. GL51 9 E5
Glebe Farm Ct. GL51 9 F6
Glebe Rd. GL52 7 F3
Glencairn Clo. GL50 9 G3
Glencairn Park Rd. GL50 9 G3
Glenfall St. GL52 6 D5
Glenfall Way. GL52 11 F3
Glenlea Gro. GL51 9 F6
Glensanda Ct. GL50 12 B6
Gloucester Pl. GL50 12 D3
Gloucester Rd. GL51 8 D3
Glynbridge Gdns. GL51 5 G4
Glyndthorpe Gro. GL51 9 F6
Glynrosa Rd. GL53 11 F4
Godfrey Clo. GL51 9 G4
Golden Miller Rd. GL50 6 B2
Golden Valley
  Bypass. GL51 8 A4
Goldsmith Rd. GL51 9 F1
Goodwin Clo. GL52 7 E5
Gordon Rd. GL53 10 B4
Grafton Rd. GL51 10 B2
Graham Pl. GL51 5 E6
Grange Walk. GL53 11 F4
Granley Clo. GL51 9 F3
Granley Dri. GL51 9 G3
Granley Rd. GL51 9 F3
Granville St. GL50 6 B4
Grasmere Rd. GL51 9 F4
Gratton Rd. GL50 10 B2
Gratton St. GL50 10 B2
Gravel Pit La. GL52 7 H2
Gravney Ct. GL51 5 F4
Great Norwood St. GL50 10 B2
Great Western Rd. GL50 6 B5
Great Western Ter. GL50 6 A5
Greatfield Dri. GL53 10 D4
Greatfield La. GL51 9 F6

Greenhills Clo. GL53 10 D4
Greenhills Rd. GL53 10 D4
Greenway La. GL51 11 F2
Grenadier Rd. GL51 5 F4
Grevil Rd. GL51 5 F4
Greville Ct. GL51 9 F3
Griffiths Av. GL51 9 G3
Grimwade Clo. GL51 9 G2
Gristmill Clo. GL51 5 E4
Grosvenor Pl Sth. GL52 12 D3
Grosvenor St. GL52 12 D4
Grosvenor Ter. GL52 12 D3
Grove St. GL50 12 A1
Grovelands Clo. GL53 11 F3
Gwernant Rd. GL51 9 F5

Hales Clo. GL52 7 E5
Hales Rd. GL52 7 E6
Hall Rd. GL53 10 B5
Halland Rd. GL53 10 B4
Hallmead Clo. GL51 5 E4
Ham Clo. GL52 11 G2
Ham Rd. GL54 11 G2
Ham Sq. GL52 11 H2
Hambrook St. GL52 11 F2
Hamilton St. GL53 11 F2
Hammond Ct. GL52 10 C2
Hampton Clo. GL51 9 H6
Hannam Clo. GL53 10 C5
*Hanover Ct, St Stephens Rd.
  GL51 10 A2
Hanover St. GL50 6 C4
Harp Hill. GL52 7 F5
Harrington Dri. GL51 9 F4
Harry Yates Way. GL51 5 E4
Hartbury Clo. GL51 4 D6
Hartlebury Way. GL52 11 G3
Hartley Clo. GL53 10 D5
Harvest Gro. GL51 5 E4
Haslette Way. GL51 9 F6
Hatherley Brake. GL51 9 E4
Hatherley Court Rd. GL51 9 H4
Hatherley Gate. GL51 9 H4
Hatherley La. GL51 8 D3
Hatherley Rd. GL51 9 E5
Hatherley St. GL50 10 A2
Hawcombe Mews. GL51 9 F6
Haweswater Rd. GL51 9 F5
Hawkswood Rd. GL51 9 H6
Hawthorn Rd. GL51 5 F6
Hayden Clo. GL51 4 B5
Hayden Rd. GL51 5 F4
Hayes Rd. GL52 7 E5
Hayscotts. GL53 10 C3
Haywards La. GL52 11 E1
Haywards Rd. GL52 11 E2
Hazebrouk Clo. GL51 9 F4
Hazelwood Clo. GL51 9 H6
Hazle Dean Rd. GL51 4 D4
Hazlitt Croft. GL51 5 E5
Heapey Clo. GL51 9 E1
Hearne Clo. GL53 11 G3
Hearne Rd. GL53 11 F3
Helens Clo. GL51 5 E5
Hendre Mws. GL51 6 A5
Henley Rd. GL51 4 D6
Henrietta St. GL50 12 B2
Hereford Pl. GL50 6 B4
Hermitage St. GL53 10 B2
Heron Clo. GL51 9 F4
Hesters Way La. GL51 5 E5
Hesters Way Rd. GL51 5 E5
Hetton Gdns. GL53 11 F2
Hewlett Pl. GL52 6 D6
Hewlett Rd. GL52 6 D6
Hicks Beach Rd. GL51 5 E6
High St. GL50 12 A1
High St. GL52 7 G2
Highbury La. GL52 12 D3
Highland Rd. GL53 10 D5
Highwood Av. GL50 10 A3
Hill Top Rd. GL53 10 C5
Hill View Rd. GL52 7 F5
Hillands Dri. GL53 10 C5
Hillary Rd. GL53 10 C5
Hillcourt Rd. GL52 6 D2
Hillfield. GL51 9 G2
Hillier Dri. GL51 9 G6
Hillside Clo. GL51 9 G4
Hine Gdns. GL52 7 E4
Hobby Clo. GL53 10 B4
Hollis Gdns. GL51 8 D5
Hollis Rd. GL51 8 D5

Home Clo. GL51 5 F5
Home Farm Ct. GL52 11 F2
Homecroft Dri. GL51 5 E3
Honeybourne Dri. GL51 5 E4
Honeysuckle Clo. GL52 7 G4
Hoopers Ct. GL52 12 B1
Hope St. GL51 6 A3
Hopwood Gro. GL52 7 E5
Horsefair St. GL53 11 E3
Howell Rd. GL51 5 F4
Hudson St. GL50 6 B3
Hulbert Clo. GL51 5 H2
Hulbert Cres. GL51 9 F6
Humber Rd. GL52 7 F5
Hungerford St. GL50 6 C4
Huntscote Rd. GL51 5 H3
Huntsfield Clo. GL50 6 D3

Idsall Dri. GL52 7 G2
Imjin Rd. GL52 7 F5
Imperial Circus. GL50 12 C3
Imperial La. GL50 12 B4
Imperial Sq. GL50 12 B4

INDUSTRIAL ESTATES:
Arle Ind Est. GL51 5 H4
Battledown
  Trading Est. GL52 11 E1
Charlton Kings
  Ind Est. GL53 11 E5
Cheltenham
  Trading Pk. GL51 5 H6
Kingsditch
  Retail Pk. GL51 5 G4
Lansdown Ind
  Est. GL51 9 G2
Manchester Park
  Ind Est. GL51 5 H5
St Johns
  Business Pk. GL51 9 H1
Shaftsbury
  Ind Est. GL51 5 H3
Isbourne Rd. GL52 7 F5
Ismay Rd. GL51 5 F5
Ivy Bank. GL52 7 G3

Jacobs Ladder. GL52 11 F1
Japonica Dri. GL51 9 G6
Jasmin Way. GL51 9 G6
Jenner Gdns. GL50 12 B2
Jenner Walk. GL50 12 B2
Jersey Av. GL52 7 E5
Jersey St. GL52 6 D5
Jessop Av. GL50 12 A2
Joyner Rd. GL51 5 G4
Juniper Ct. GL51 8 D1
Justica Way. GL51 9 G6

Keire Walk. GL51 5 G4
Kemerton Rd. GL50 9 H5
Kempton Gro. GL51 8 D1
Kenelm Dri. GL53 10 B3
Kenelm Gdns. GL53 10 A3
Kenneth Clo. GL53 10 C5
Kensington Av. GL50 9 H3
Kentmere Clo. GL51 9 F4
Kerstin Clo. GL50 6 B2
Kestrel Clo. GL51 10 B4
Keswick Rd. GL51 9 F4
Kew Pl. GL53 10 C2
Keynsham Bank. GL52 10 D1
Keynsham Rd. GL53 10 D2
Keynsham St. GL52 10 D1
Keynshambury Rd.
  GL52 10 D1
Kidnappers La. GL53 10 A5
Kimberley Walk. GL52 7 G5
King Alfred Way. GL51 11 E1
King Arthur Clo. GL51 11 E2
King George Clo. GL53 10 D3
King Henry Clo. GL53 10 D3
King St. GL50 6 B5
King William Rd. GL53 10 D3
Kings Rd. GL52 7 E6
Kingscote Av. GL51 9 E4
Kingscote Clo. GL51 9 E4
Kingscote Gro. GL51 9 E4
Kingscote Rd E. GL51 9 E4
Kingscote Rd W. GL51 9 E5
Kingsditch La. GL51 5 H4
Kingsditch Retail Pk.
  GL51 5 G4
Kingsley Gdns. GL51 9 F2
Kingsmead Av. GL51 5 F5

Kingsmead Clo. GL51 5 G5
Kingsmead Rd. GL51 5 G5
Kingston Clo. GL51 8 D2
Kingsville Rd. GL51 5 H4
Kipling Rd. GL51 9 F2
Knapp La. GL50 12 A2
Knapp Rd. GL50 12 A2
Knightsbridge Cres. GL53 11 E2

Laburnum Ct. GL51 8 D1
Ladysmith Rd. GL52 7 G4
Lake St. GL52 7 F2
Landor Gdns. GL52 7 E5
Langdale Rd. GL51 9 G4
Langdon Rd. GL53 10 B3
Langton Grove Rd. GL51 11 E2
Langton Pl. GL53 11 E2
Lansdown Castle Dri.
  GL51 9 G3
Lansdown Clo. GL51 9 G3
Lansdown Cres. GL50 10 A1
Lansdown Cres La.
  GL50 10 A1
Lansdown Ind Est. GL51 9 G2
Lansdown Lodge Dri.
  GL51 9 H3
Lansdown Par. GL50 10 A1
Lansdown Pl. GL50 10 A1
Lansdown Pl La. GL50 10 A1
Lansdown Rd. GL51 10 A1
Lansdown Ter La. GL50 6 B6
Lansdown Walk. GL50 10 A1
Larch Clo. GL53 11 G4
Larchmere Gro. GL51 9 F6
Larput Pl. GL50 6 C4
Laurel Dri. GL50 7 F3
Lavender Rd. GL51 9 G6
Lawrence Clo. GL52 11 G3
Lawson Glade. GL53 11 E4
Laxton Rd. GL51 9 F1
Laxton Walk. GL51 9 F1
Lechmere Rd. GL51 5 F6
Leckhampton Farm Ct.
  GL51 10 A5
Leckhampton La. GL51 10 A6
Leckhampton Rd. GL53 10 B3
Ledmore Rd. GL53 11 F3
Lee Clo. GL51 5 G5
Leighton Rd. GL52 6 D6
Leinster Clo. GL51 4 D5
Lewis Rd. GL51 9 E1
Leyson Rd. GL51 8 C4
Libertus Ct. GGL51 9 G2
Libertus Rd. GL51 9 G2
Lichfield Dri. GL51 9 H6
Liddington Clo. GL51 10 C5
Liddington Rd. GL53 10 C5
Lilac Clo. GL51 9 G6
Limber Hill. GL50 6 B2
Lime Clo. GL52 7 E2
Lincoln Dri. GL51 9 G6
Linden Av. GL52 7 E2
Linden Clo. GL52 7 F2
Linton Ct. GL53 10 C2
Linwell Clo. GL50 6 A2
Lipson Rd. GL51 5 F5
Little Bayshill Ter. GL50 12 A3
Little Cleevemount. GL52 6 D3
Little Herberts Clo. GL53 11 F4
Little Herberts Rd. GL53 11 F4
Littledown Rd. GL53 10 D5
London Rd. GL52 11 E2
Long Mynd Av. GL51 9 E5
Longway Av. GL51 11 E5
Lower Mill St. GL51 6 A4
Loweswater Clo. GL51 9 G4
Loweswater Rd. GL51 9 G4
Lyfield Clo. GL53 11 F3
Lyfield Rd East. GL53 11 F3
Lyfield Rd West. GL53 11 F3
Lygon Walk. GL51 5 G5
Lyndale Ter. GL51 9 H1
Lynworth Pl. GL52 7 F4
Lypiatt Dri. GL50 10 B1
Lypiatt Rd. GL50 10 B1
Lypiatt St. GL50 10 A2

Mackenzie Way. GL51 5 G3
Magnolia Clo. GL51 8 D1
Maidavale Rd. GL53 10 C3
Malden Rd. GL52 6 D4
Malmesbury Rd. GL51 5 G4
Malthouse La. GL50 6 C4

Malvern Pl. GL50 6
Malvern Rd. GL50 6
Malvern St. GL51 6
Manchester Park
  Ind Est. GL51 5
Mandarin Way. GL50 5
Manor Ct. GL51 5
Manor Rd. GL51 5
Manse Gdns. GL51 9
Manser St. GL50 6
Maple Dri. GL53 11
Marchant Clo. GL51 5
Margrett Rd. GL50 6
Market St. GL50 6
Marle Hill Par. GL50 6
Marle Hill Rd. GL50 6
Marsh Clo. GL51 6
Marsh Dri. GL51 6
Marsh Gdns. GL51 6
Marsh La. GL51 6
Marsland Rd. GL51 6
Marston Rd. GL51 6
Maythorn Dri. GL51 5
Mead Clo. GL53 10
Mead Rd. GL53 10
Meadow Clo. GL50 8
Meadow La. GL51 9
Medoc Clo. GL50 6
Melbourne Clo. GL53 10
Mendip Clo. GL52 7
Mendip Rd. GL52 7
Merestones Clo. GL50 10
Merestones Dri. GL50 10
Merestones Rd. GL50 10
Merlin Way. GL53 10
Merriville Gdns. GL51 5
Merriville Rd. GL51 5
Mersey Rd. GL52 7
Midwinter Av. GL50 6
Midwinter Clo. GL50 6
Mill House Dri. GL50 6
Mill La, Ham. GL52 11
Mill La, Prestbury. GL52 7
Mill St. GL52
Millbrook Gdns. GL50 6
Millbrook St. GL50 6
Milsom St. GL50 6
Milton Av. GL51
Milton Rd. GL51
Mimosa Av. GL51 9
Miserden Rd. GL51 9
Mitre St. GL53 12
Monica Dri. GL51
Monkscroft. GL51
Monson Av. GL50 12
Montgomery Rd. GL51
Montpellier Arc. GL50 12
Montpellier Av. GL50 12
Montpellier Dri. GL50 1
Montpellier Gro. GL50 10
Montpellier Par. GL50 1
Montpellier Spa Rd.
  GL50 1
Montpellier St. GL50 12
Montpellier Ter. GL50 12
Montpellier Villas. GL50 1
Montpellier Walk. GL50 1
Moor Court Dri. GL52
Moorend Cres. GL53 1
Moorend Glade. GL53 1
Moorend Gro. GL53 1
Moorend Park Rd. GL53 1
Moorend Rd,
  Leckhampton. GL53 1
Moorend Rd,
  Moor End. GL53 1
Moorend St. GL53 1
Moors Av. GL51
Morlands Dri. GL53 1
Morningside Ct Yd. GL52
Mornington Dri. GL53 1
Morris Ct. GL51
Morris Hill Clo. GL51
Mulberry Ct. GL51
Murvagh Clo. GL53 1
Muscroft Rd. GL52

Naunton Cres. GL53 1
Naunton La. GL53 1
Naunton Par..GL53 1
Naunton Park Clo. GL53 1
Naunton Park Rd. GL53 1
Naunton Ter. GL53

32

mmercial Rd. GL1 13 B3
mpton Clo. GL3 16 D1
ncorde Way. GL4 19 G5
nduit St. GL1 19 E4
ney Hill Par. GL4 19 H5
ney Hill Rd. GL4 19 G4
niston Rd. GL2 15 H5
nstitution Walk. GL1 13 D4
nway Rd. GL3 20 D4
oks Orchard. GL1 15 E6
ppers Elm. GL2 22 C4
ppers Vw. GL3 26 B2
pper Beech Gro. GL2 22 B4
pperfield Clo. GL4 24 B1
ppice Mews. GL4 20 D4
al Clo. GL4 23 E3
dingley Clo. GL3 17 F5
iander Dri. GL3 16 C3
ncroft La. GL4 24 C3
nfield Dri. GL2 26 B3
nflower Rd. GL4 20 B6
olin Rd. GL2 22 D2
onation Grove. GL2 19 G2
swold Gdns. GL2 16 A4
teswold Rd. GL4 19 F6
ton Clo. GL4 25 F1
rt Gdns. GL2 18 A5
rt Pl. GL4 20 A5
rt Rd. GL3 26 B2
rtfield Rd. GL2 22 B5
sley Clo. GL3 20 D5
wley Rd. GL4 23 G3
's Way. GL4 20 C6
more Clo. GL3 20 D4
nham Clo. GL4 25 E1
nham La. GL3 17 F6
nwell Clo. GL4 24 C2
ven Dri. GL3 16 D3
ton Rd. GL3 20 B3
scentdale. GL2 15 F3
st Way. GL4 20 C2
ycraft La. GL3 17 F6
pin Clo. GL3 15 H4
t Clo. GL3 17 F5
nwell St. GL1 18 D3
ss Keys La. GL1 13 C3
ot Ct. GL3 23 E2
ew Rd. GL4 19 H6
is Hayward Dri. GL2 22 B4

odil Clo. GL4 20 B6
aty St. GL1 19 E4
e Clo. GL4 23 H1
ason Clo. GL4 25 E1
cey Rd. GL3 16 C3
e Clo. GL4 15 H4
et Clo. GL2 20 C6
vin Rd. GL4 24 A1
ns Ter. GL1 14 D6
ns Walk. GL1 14 D6
ns Way. GL1 14 D6
Park Rd. GL3 20 D3
hurst Clo. GL4 25 E2
hurst Pl. GL2 22 A5
ham Clo. GL4 23 E4
mark Rd. GL1 15 E6
ay Ct. GL1 19 F3
ay Rd. GL1 19 F3
vent Clo. GL3 26 B2
ord Clo. GL4 25 F1
erdale Dri. GL2 16 A5
ding Way. GL3 17 F4
ny Clo. GL2 22 B4
e Clo. GL3 16 C2
ton Way. GL4 24 C1
vs Clo. GL3 17 F5
vs Court. GL3 17 F5
moor. GL4 24 D2
s Oak. GL2 22 B4
Meadow La. GL3 15 H2
e Clo. GL3 19 E4

Duke of Beaufort Ct. GL1 23 F1
Duncroft Rd. GL3 20 C2
Dunlin Clo. GL2 22 A4
Dunstan Glen. GL3 17 F5
Dunster Clo. GL4 23 E4
Durand Clo. GL2 15 H3
Durham Rd. GL4 19 H3
Dynevor St. GL1 19 E4

Eagle Way. GL4 19 H6
Eardisland Rd. GL4 23 G3
East Cott Way. GL3 16 D3
Eastbrook Rd. GL4 19 H3
Eastern Av. GL4 19 G5
Eastgate St. GL1 13 D3
Eastville Clo. GL4 19 G4
Ebor Rd. GL2 19 H2
Edgeworth Clo. GL4 25 E1
Edwy Par. GL1 14 D6
Elderberry Mws. GL3 16 C3
Eldersfield Clo. GL2 22 A4
Elderwood Way. GL4 23 E3
Eliot Clo. GL2 23 E2
Ellesmere Clo. GL3 20 C3
Ellison Clo. GL4 20 D6
Elm Dri. GL3 21 G5
Elmbridge Ct. GL3 16 B5
Elmbridge Rd. GL2 19 H2
Elmgrove Est. GL2 26 B3
Elmgrove Rd. GL3 20 C5
Elmgrove Rd East. GL2 26 C3
Elmgrove Rd West. GL2 22 A6
Elmira Rd. GL4 23 G1
Elmleaze. GL2 16 A6
Elmore La. GL2 22 A3
Emerald Way. GL2 23 E2
Empire Way. GL2 18 B6
Enborne Clo. GL4 23 F4
Ennerdale Av. GL2 15 H4
Epney Rd. GL2 23 E2
Ermin Pk. GL3 21 F5
Ermin St. GL3 21 F5
Erminster Dri. GL3 20 C4
Essex Clo. GL3 16 C1
Estcourt Clo. GL1 15 F5
Estcourt Rd. GL1 15 E5
Etheridge Pl. GL1 19 F2
Evans Walk. GL4 24 B1
Evenlode Rd. GL4 23 F4

Forest View Rd. GL4 23 G4
Forsyte Way. GL4 19 G5
Fosse Clo. GL4 20 B5
Fourth Av. GL4 23 F3
Fox Clo. GL4 20 C6
Fox Elms Rd. GL4 23 G3
Foxcote. GL2 15 G4
Foxglove Clo. GL4 20 B6
Foxleigh Cres. GL4 16 B4
Foxtail Clo. GL4 24 A1
Foxwell Dri. GL3 20 C4
Frampton Rd. GL1 18 C4
Fretherne Rd. GL4 23 F2
Friary Rd. GL4 20 B5
Frobisher Mews. GL3 16 C1
Frog Furlong La. GL2 16 B1
Fullers Ct. GL1 13 B2
Furlong Rd. GL1 18 D4
Furze Croft. GL2 22 B6

Gainsborough Dri. GL4 23 E4
Gambier Parry Gdns. GL2 15 E5
Gannet Clo. GL3 26 B2
Garden Way. GL2 15 G5
Gardiners Clo. GL3 16 D3
Garnalls Rd. GL4 24 C2
Gatmeres Rd. GL4 24 C3
Gatton Way. GL3 20 C2
George St. GL1 13 F3
George Whitfield Clo. GL4 24 C1
Georgian Clo. GL4 25 E2
Gere Clo. GL4 23 F4
Gibson Rd. GL3 15 H4
Gifford Clo. GL2 15 H4
Gilbert Rd. GL2 15 G4
Giles Cox. GL2 22 B5
Gilpin Av. GL3 20 C2
Gimson Clo. GL4 23 F4
Gladiator Clo. GL4 23 F4
Gladstone Rd. GL1 18 C5
Glencairn Av. GL4 23 E5
Glendower Clo. GL3 16 C1
Glenville Par. GL3 20 D4
Glevum Clo. GL2 15 G5
Glevum Way. GL4 24 D1
Gloucester M5 Southern
  Connector. GL2 22 C6
Gloucester Northern
  By-Pass. GL3 14 B5
Gloucester
  Trading Est. GL3 21 E6
Goddard Way. GL4 23 F4
Golden Clo. GL4 23 E3
Golden Vale. GL3 17 E3
Golden Valley
  By-Pass. GL3 16 B4
Goldsborough Clo. GL4 19 G5
Golf Club La. GL3 21 F5
Goodmore Cres. GL3 16 B3
Goodridge Av. GL2 22 C2
Goodyere St. GL1 19 E3
Gorse Clo. GL4 25 F1
Goss Wood Corner. GL2 22 A5
Gothic Cott. GL1 19 F3
Grafton Rd. GL2 19 G1
Graham Gdns. GL1 15 F6
Grange Rd. GL4 23 E3
Granville St. GL1 18 C5
Grasby Clo. GL4 20 B4
Grasmere Rd. GL2 15 H5
Gray Clo. GL3 16 B2
Great Western Rd. GL1 13 F2
Grebe Clo. GL4 24 D1
Green Acre. GL3 26 B2
Green Bank. GL3 26 B2
Green Clo. GL3 26 B2
Green Gdns. GL3 26 B2
Green La,
  Brockworth. GL3 26 D1
Green La,
  Churchdown. GL3 17 F5
Green La,
  Hardwicke. GL3 26 B3
Green La,
  Hucclecote. GL3 20 D5
Green Way. GL3 26 A2
Green Way. GL3 26 B2
Greenhill Clo. GL4 22 D3
Greenhill Dri. GL4 22 D3
Greenville Clo. GL3 16 C1
Greenwood Clo. GL3 21 E5

Grenadier Clo. GL4 20 C5
Greyfriars. GL1 13 C4
Greyhound Gdns. GL2 16 B4
Greyling Clo. GL4 25 E1
Grisedale Clo. GL2 15 H4
Grosvenor Rd. GL2 19 G1
Grove Cres. GL4 20 A2
Grove Rd. GL3 16 C4
Grove St. GL1 19 E4
Grovelands. GL4 20 B3
Guinea St. GL1 15 E6
Guise Av. GL3 26 C2
Guise Clo. GL2 22 B5
Gurney Av. GL4 23 F4

Hadow Way. GL2 22 B6
Hadrian Way. GL4 20 B5
Hailes Rd. GL4 20 A5
Hamer St. GL1 19 F2
Hammond Way. GL4 20 A2
Hampden Way. GL1 13 D4
Hampton Clo. GL3 21 E4
Hampton Pl. GL3 16 D1
Hanman Rd. GL1 19 E4
Hannah Pl. GL3 16 B2
Hanover Way. GL3 16 C2
Harbury Mews. GL1 19 F3
Hare La. GL1 13 D2
Harebell Pl. GL4 20 B6
Haresfield La. GL4 26 C4
Harewood Clo. GL3 23 E4
Harris Clo. GL3 17 E4
Hartington Rd. GL1 18 C5
Hartland Rd. GL1 19 E6
Harvest Way. GL2 22 B6
Harvey Clo. GL2 23 E1
Hasfield Clo. GL2 22 A4
Hatfield Rd. GL1 19 F4
Hathaway Clo. GL2 23 E2
Hatherley Rd. GL1 19 E5
Havelock Rd. GL3 20 D3
Haven Ct. GL2 19 H1
Hawk Clo. GL4 20 A6
Hawthorn Dri. GL3 16 C3
Hawthorne Av. GL4 19 H6
Haycroft Dri. GL4 24 D3
Haydale Gdns. GL2 15 H4
Hayes Ct. GL2 15 E3
Hazel Clo. GL2 15 G4
Hazelcroft. GL3 16 D3
Headlam Clo. GL4 23 F4
Heath Dean Rd. GL3 16 C3
Heather Av. GL4 25 F1
Heathville Rd. GL1 15 E6
Hebden Clo. GL2 26 C2
Hembury Clo. GL2 22 A6
Hemmingsdale Rd. GL2 18 B3
Hempsted La. GL2 18 A5
Hendingham Clo. GL4 22 D3
Henley Pl. GL1 18 D6
Henry Rd. GL1 19 E1
Henry St. GL1 19 E1
Herbert St. GL1 19 F3
Heron Way. GL4 19 H6
Hethersett Rd. GL1 19 F3
Hickley Gdns. GL3 26 B1
High Orchard St. GL1 18 C3
High St. GL1 19 E4
High St. GL4 25 E4
High View. GL2 18 A5
Highbank Pk. GL2 15 E4
Highclere Rd. GL4 22 A4
Highfield Rd. GL4 19 G5
Highgrove Way. GL3 16 C2
Highliffe Dri. GL2 22 C5
Highworth Rd. GL1 19 E5
Hildyard Clo. GL4 26 C3
Hill Hay Rd. GL4 24 C3
Hillborough Rd. GL4 23 G3
Hillcot Clo. GL2 22 A4
Hillfield Court Rd. GL1 19 F1
Hillview Av. GL3 21 F5
Hillview Dri. GL3 20 C3
Hillview Rd. GL3 20 C3
Hilton Clo. GL2 18 A5
Hinton Rd. GL1 15 E5
Holham Av. GL3 17 E2
Holly End. GL2 22 C5
Holmleigh Rd. GL4 23 F4
Holmwood Clo. GL4 23 F4
Holmwood Dri. GL4 23 F4
Holst Way. GL4 23 F3

Homestead Ct. GL4 25 E1
Honeysuckle Dri. GL4 20 B6
Honeythorne Clo. GL2 18 A4
Honyatt Rd. GL1 19 E1
Hooper Clo. GL4 19 G5
Hopewell St. GL1 19 E3
Hornbeam Mews. GL2 15 G4
Horsebere Rd. GL3 20 D3
Horsley Clo. GL4 25 E1
Horton Rd. GL1 19 F2
*Howard Pl,
  Hucclecote Rd. GL3 20 D4
Howard St. GL1 18 D4
Howcroft. GL3 17 F5
Howgate Clo. GL4 20 C6
Hucclecote Rd. GL3 20 B3
Humber Pl. GL3 26 C2
Hunters Gate. GL4 24 D2
Huntley Clo. GL4 20 B6
Hurcombe Way. GL3 26 B1
Hurran Gdns. GL3 16 D2
Hurst Clo. GL2 16 A4
Huxley Rd. GL1 19 E5
Hyde Clo. GL1 19 F1
Hyde La. GL1 19 E1

India Rd. GL1 19 F3
INDUSTRIAL ESTATES:
  Gloucester
    Trading Est. GL3 21 E6
  Innsworth
    Technology Pk. GL3 15 H3
  Morelands
    Trading Est. GL1 18 C4
  St Oswalds
    Trading Est. GL1 14 D5
Innsworth La. GL2 15 H3
Innsworth
  Technology Pk. GL3 15 H3
Insley Gdns. GL3 20 B3
Ivory Clo. GL4 23 E3

Jackson Cres. GL3 16 B3
James Grieve Rd. GL4 20 C6
James Way. GL3 21 E5
Jasmine Clo. GL4 24 D2
Javelin Way. GL3 26 B2
Jaythorpe. GL4 24 D2
Jenner Clo. GL3 20 C4
Jennings Walk. GL1 13 D4
Jersey Rd. GL1 19 E3
Jewson Clo. GL4 23 F4
John Daniels Way. GL3 17 F5
John Woods Alley. GL1 15 E6
Jordans Way. GL2 15 E4
Julian Clo. GL4 20 A3
Juniper Av. GL4 24 B2
Jupiter Way. GL4 20 C5

Katherine Clo. GL3 16 C1
Kaybourne Cres. GL3 17 G4
Keats Av. GL2 23 E2
Kemble Clo. GL4 23 F3
Kemble Rd. GL4 23 G2
Kencourt Clo. GL2 19 G1
Kendal Rd. GL2 15 H6
Kenilworth Av. GL2 19 F1
Kennedy Clo. GL3 20 C3
Kennet Gdns. GL4 25 E2
Kent Clo. GL3 17 G4
Kenton Dri. GL3 15 H4
Keriston Av. GL3 16 D3
Keswick Clo. GL2 15 G6
Kevin Clo. GL4 20 A3
Kew Pl. GL2 15 H4
Kilminster Ct. GL3 16 D3
Kimberley Clo. GL2 16 A5
Kimbrose Way. GL1 13 C4
King Edwards Av. GL1 18 D5
Kingfisher Rise. GL2 22 A5
Kings Barton St. GL1 18 E2
Kings Sq. GL1 13 E1
Kings Walk. GL1 13 D3
Kingscote Clo. GL3 17 G5
Kingscote Dri. GL4 25 E1
Kingscroft Rd. GL3 20 C4
Kingsholm Ct. GL1 14 D5
Kingsholm Rd. GL1 15 E6
Kingsholm Sq. GL1 14 D6
Kingsley Rd. GL4 19 F6
Kingsmead. GL4 25 E1
Kingstone Av. GL3 20 B3
Kinmoor. GL4 24 D2

Kitchener Av. GL1 18 D6
Knollys End. GL2 22 B5
Knowles Rd. GL1 19 E4

Laburnum Gdns. GL2 22 B4
Laburnum Rd. GL1 23 F1
Lacca Clo. GL2 16 A4
Lacy Clo. GL2 15 H3
Lady Chapel Rd. GL4 20 B5
Ladybellegate St. GL1 13 B3
Ladysmith Rd. GL1 18 D6
Ladywell Clo. GL2 18 A5
Langdale Gdns. GL2 16 B6
Langley Rd. GL4 24 B1
Langton Clo. GL3 20 B3
Lanham Gdns. GL2 22 B6
Lannett Rd. GL1 18 D5
Lansdown Rd. GL1 15 E6
Larchwood Dri. GL4 23 G2
Larkham Clo. GL4 24 B3
Larkham Pl. GL4 24 C3
Larkhay Rd. GL3 20 D4
Larkspear Clo. GL1 18 D6
Lasne Cres. GL3 26 C2
Laura Clo. GL2 15 G5
Laurel Gate. GL4 25 F1
Lavender Vw. GL4 25 F1
Lavington Dri. GL2 16 B5
Lawrence Way. GL2 14 D6
Lawrence Way Nth. GL2 14 C5
Laxton Rd. GL4 20 D5
Laynes Rd. GL3 20 D4
Lea Cres. GL2 15 H4
Lea Rd. GL3 26 C2
Leacey Ct. GL3 16 D2
Leacey Mews. GL3 16 D2
Leadon Clo. GL3 26 C2
Leonard Rd. GL1 19 E5
Leven Clo. GL2 16 A5
Lewis Av. GL2 15 E3
Lewisham Rd. GL1 18 D6
Lichfield Rd. GL4 19 H3
Liddington Rd. GL2 16 B6
Lilac Way. GL4 23 E3
Lilac Way. GL2 22 B4
Lilliesfield Av. GL3 20 B3
Linden Rd. GL1 18 C5
Linnet Clo. GL4 24 C1
Linsley Way. GL4 23 F4
Little Awefield. GL4 24 C1
Little Elmbridge. GL2 16 A5
Little Normans. GL2 15 H4
Little Walk. GL2 .15 H4
Littlefield. GL2 22 B4
Llandilo St. GL1 19 E4
Llanthony Rd. GL1 18 C2
Lobleys Dri. GL4 20 C6
London Rd. GL1 13 E2
Long Hope Clo. GL4 20 B6
Longborough Dri. GL4 20 B6
Longfield. GL2 22 B4
Longford La. GL2 15 E3
Longford Mews. GL2 15 E2
Longland Ct. GL2 15 G4
Longlands Gdns. GL2 15 G5
Longleat Av. GL4 23 E5
Longney Rd. GL2 23 F2
Longsmith St. GL1 13 C3
Longville Clo. GL4 25 F1
Lonsdale Rd. GL2 19 H1
Loriners Clo. GL2 22 B4
Lower Meadow. GL2 22 B6
Lower Quay St. GL1 13 B2
Lower Tuffley La. GL2 22 D2
Luke La. GL3 16 B3
Lyng Clo. GL4 20 B3
Lynmouth Rd. GL3 20 C5
Lynton Rd. GL3 20 C5
Lysander Ct. GL3 17 F4
Lysons Av. GL1 18 C5

Madleaze Rd. GL1 18 C4
Magdala Rd. GL1 19 E3
Mainard Sq. GL2 15 G4
Maisemore Rd. GL2 14 A2
Maldon Gdns. GL1 19 E5
Malet Clo. GL2 15 H4
Mallard Clo. GL2 22 A4
Malmesbury Rd. GL4 19 F4
Malvern Rd. GL1 15 E5
Mandara Gro. GL4 24 D2
Mandeville Clo. GL2 15 H4

Manley Gdns. GL2 15 G4
Manor Gdns. GL4 20 B3
Manor Pk. GL2 16 B5
Mansell Clo. GL2 23 E1
Mansfield Mews. GL2 22 B6
Maple Clo. GL2 22 A6
Maple Dri. GL2 21 F4
Marefield Clo. GL4 20 B4
Marjoram Clo. GL4 20 C6
Marian Ct. GL1 13 B1
Market Par. GL1 13 E3
Market Way. GL1 13 D3
Marlborough Cres. GL4 19 F5
Marlborough Rd. GL4 19 F5
Marleyfield Clo. GL3 16 D2
Marleyfield Way. GL3 16 D2
Marram Clo. GL4 20 C6
Marsden Rd. GL3 16 C3
Marten Clo. GL4 20 C6
Martindale Rd. GL3 16 D3
Marwell Clo. GL4 23 F5
Mary Rose Av. GL3 16 C2
Marylone. GL1 13 C3
Masefield Av. GL2 23 E1
Massey Pde. GL2 19 E5
Massey Rd. GL1 19 F5
Matson Av. GL4 24 C1
Matson La. GL4 24 B2
Matson Pl. GL1 19 F5
Maverdine Pass. GL1 13 C3
Mayall Ct. GL4 24 C3
Mayfair Clo. GL2 18 B4
Mayfield Dri. GL3 20 C3
Maytree Sq. GL4 19 H5
Mead Rd. GL4 20 B6
Meadow Way. GL3 17 E3
Meadowcroft. GL4 20 B6
Meadowleaze. GL2 16 A6
Meadvale Clo. GL2 15 E3
Medway Cres. GL3 26 C2
Meerstone Way. GL4 24 D2
Melbourne St East. GL1 19 E4
Melbourne St West. GL1 19 E4
Melick Clo. GL4 24 A1
Melody Way. GL2 16 B4
Melville Rd. GL3 17 E4
Mendip Clo. GL2 22 A5
Merchants Mead. GL2 22 A5
Merchants Rd. GL1 18 C3
Mercia Rd. GL1 14 D6
Mercury Way. GL4 20 C5
Merevale Rd. GL2 15 G6
Meteor Way. GL3 26 B2
Metz Way. GL1 19 E2
Michaelmas Ct. GL1 15 F6
Middleton Lawn. GL3 16 B3
Midland Rd. GL1 18 D4
Milford Clo. GL2 15 G4
Mill Gro. GL2 22 A5
Mill La. GL3 26 B1
Mill St. GL1 19 F3
Millbridge Rd. GL3 20 D4
Millbrook Clo. GL1 19 F3
Millbrook St. GL1 19 E3
Miller Clo. GL2 16 A4
Millers Dyke. GL2 22 A5
Millers Grn. GL1 13 C2
Millfields. GL3 20 D3
Millin Av. GL2 23 F3
Milo Pl. GL1 18 D5
Milton Av. GL2 23 E1
Minerva Clo. GL4 20 C5
Minster Gdns. GL4 20 B5
Minstrel Way. GL3 16 C1
Mogride Clo. GL3 20 D4
Monarch Clo. GL4 25 E1
Monk Meadow. GL2 18 B4
Montford Rd. GL2 15 G4
Montgomery Clo. GL3 21 E5
Montpellier. GL1 18 D3
Montpellier Mews. GL1 18 D3
Moor St. GL1 19 E4
Moorfield Rd. GL3 26 B2
Morelands Trading Est. GL1 18 C4
Morley Av. GL3 16 D3
Morpeth St. GL1 19 E4
Mortimer Rd. GL4 19 E4
Morton St. GL1 19 E4
Morton Cotts. GL1 19 E3
Morwent Clo. GL4 20 B6
Mosselle Dri. GL3 16 D3
Mottershead Dri. GL3 16 B2

Mount St. GL1 13 B1
Mowberry Clo. GL2 15 H4
Mulberry Clo. GL2 22 A6
Munsley Gro. GL4 24 C3
Mutsilver Mews. GL2 16 B4
Myers Rd. GL1 19 F2
Myrtle Clo. GL4 24 B1

Naas La. GL4 22 C6
Napier St. GL1 19 E2
Naunton Rd. GL4 20 A5
Nelson St. GL1 19 E5
Neptune Clo. GL4 20 C5
Netheridge Clo. GL2 22 C1
Nettleton Rd. GL1 13 E4
New Inn La. GL1 13 D3
New St. GL1 18 D4
Newark Rd. GL1 18 B5
Newland St. GL1 19 E1
Newstead Rd. GL4 20 B3
Newton Av. GL4 19 G5
Nine Elms Rd. GL2 15 H4
Noak Rd. GL3 21 G5
Noake Rd. GL3 20 D4
Norbury Av. GL4 24 B1
Norfolk St. GL1 18 C3
Norman Ball Way. GL1 19 F2
North Rd. GL1 15 E5
North Upton La. GL3 20 B4
Northbrook Rd. GL4 19 H2
Northfield Rd. GL4 19 H2
Northfield Sq. GL4 19 E6
Northgate St. GL1 13 D3
Notgrove Clo. GL4 23 E3
Notley Pl. GL3 20 D4
Nutley Av. GL4 23 E4
Nutmeg Clo. GL4 24 D2
Nympsfield Rd. GL4 23 F3

Oak Bank. GL4 23 G2
Oak Croft Clo. GL4 24 D3
Oak Dri. GL3 21 G5
Oak Tree Clo. GL2 26 B3
Oak Tree Gdn. GL4 24 C2
Oakhurst Clo. GL3 16 C4
Oakleaze. GL2 16 A6
Oakridge Clo. GL4 25 E1
Oakwood Dri. GL3 20 C5
Oatfield. GL2 22 B4
Old Cheltenham Rd. GL2 15 H5
Old Painswick Rd. GL4 19 G5
Old Row. GL1 19 E3
Old Tram Rd. GL1 18 D3
Oldbury Orchard. GL3 17 F5
Orchard Clo, Hardwicke. GL2 26 B3
Orchard Clo, Walham. GL2 14 D4
Orchard Dri. GL2 17 F5
Orchard Rd. GL2 16 B5
Orchard Way. GL3 17 E2
Organs Alley. GL1 13 E4
Oriole Way. GL4 20 A5
Osborne Av. GL4 23 E4
Osbourne Clo. GL2 16 B6
Osier Clo. GL4 24 A1
Osprey Clo. GL4 20 A6
Osric Rd. GL1 19 E5
Otter Rd. GL4 20 C6
Over Causeway. GL2 14 A5
Overbridge Path. GL2 14 A6
Overbrook Clo. GL4 19 H3
Overbrook Rd. GL2 22 A6
Overbury Rd. GL1 19 F3
Owl Clo. GL4 20 A6
Oxford Rd. GL1 15 E6
Oxford St. GL1 13 F1
Oxford Ter. GL4 13 F2
Oxmoor. GL4 24 D2
Oxstalls Dri. GL2 15 F4
Oxstalls La. GL2 15 G6
Oxstalls Way. GL2 15 G5

Paddock Gdns. GL2 15 H4
Painswick Rd, Brockworth. GL4 26 C2
Painswick Rd, Saintbridge. GL4 19 G5
Palmer Av. GL4 25 F1
Park Av. GL2 15 H4
Park Dri. GL2 22 B5
Park Rd. GL2 18 D3
Park St. GL1 19 E4

Parkend Rd. GL1 18 D4
Parklands. GL3 22 B5
Parkside Clo. GL3 16 C3
Parkside Dri. GL3 16 C3
Parkwood Cres. GL3 20 C5
Parliament St. GL1 13 C4
Parr Clo. GL3 16 C2
Parry Rd. GL1 19 E5
Parton Dri. GL4 17 F4
Parton Rd. GL3 16 D2
Partridge Clo. GL2 23 E1
Patseamur Mews. GL2 16 B4
Paul St. GL1 19 E4
Paygrove La. GL2 16 A5
Paynes Pitch. GL3 17 F5
Peacock Clo. GL4 25 E1
Pear Tree Clo. GL2 26 B3
Pearce Way. GL2 22 D1
Peart Clo. GL2 19 F2
Pearwood Way. GL4 23 E3
Pelham Cres. GL3 16 D3
Pembroke St. GL1 19 E3
Pembury Rd. GL4 23 G1
Pendock Clo. GL2 22 A4
Penhill Rd. GL4 24 B1
Pennine Clo. GL2 22 A6
Penny Clo. GL2 16 A5
Penrose Rd. GL3 16 A3
Percy St. GL1 19 E4
Perry Orchard. GL4 25 E4
Petworth Clo. GL4 23 E5
Philip St. GL1 18 C4
Piggy La. GL4 23 G4
Pilgrim Clo. GL4 20 B5
Pillcroft Clo. GL2 26 D2
Pillcroft Rd. GL3 26 D2
Pine Tree Drive. GL3 20 B4
Pinemount Rd. GL3 20 D4
Pinery Rd. GL4 20 B4
Pineway. GL4 19 G6
Pinewood Rd. GL2 22 A6
Pinlocks. GL4 25 E3
Pippin Clo. GL4 20 D6
Pirton Cres. GL3 17 E4
Pirton La. GL3 16 C3
Pirton Mdw. GL3 16 D4
Pitt Mill Gdns. GL3 20 D3
Pitt St. GL1 13 C1
Plock Ct. GL2 15 E4
Plum Tree Clo. GL4 25 E1
Podsmead Pl. GL1 18 C6
Podsmead Rd. GL1 23 F2
Poplar Clo. GL3 23 F1
Poplar Way. GL2 26 B3
Porchester Rd. GL3 20 C4
Portway. GL4 25 F5
Pound Clo. GL2 26 B2
Pound La. GL2 26 A4
Prescott Av. GL4 24 B1
Price St. GL1 18 C4
Primrose Clo. GL4 24 A1
Prince Albert Ct. GL3 21 F5
Prince St. GL1 13 F4
Prinknash Clo. GL4 24 C1
Prinknash Rd. GL4 24 C2
Priory Pl. GL1 13 C4
Priory Rd. GL1 13 C1
Purcell Rd. GL3 16 C1
Purslane Clo. GL4 24 B1

Quail Clo. GL4 20 B4
Quantock Clo. GL4 22 A6
Quay St. GL1 13 B2
Queens Clo. GL3 20 D3
Queens Walk. GL1 13 D4
Quenneys Clo. GL4 24 C3
Quinton Clo. GL3 17 E3

Raglan St. GL1 19 E3
Raikes Rd. GL1 18 D5
Raleigh Clo. GL3 16 C1
Ramsdale Rd. GL2 22 D2
Rance Pitch. GL4 25 E3
Randwick Rd. GL4 23 F3
Ranmoor. GL4 24 D3
Ravis Clo. GL4 19 G5
Rea La. GL2 18 A5
Rectory La. GL2 18 A5
Rectory Rd. GL4 24 C2
Red Admiral Dri. GL4 25 E1
Red Poll Way. GL4 19 H6
Red Well Rd. GL4 24 C3
Redding Clo. GL2 22 A4

Redland Clo. GL2 15
Redstart Way. GL4 19
Redwind Way. GL2 16
Redwood Clo. GL1 23
Regent St. GL1 19
Remus Clo. GL4 20
Rendcomb Clo. GL4 25
Reservoir Rd, Saintbridge. GL4 19
Reservoir Rd, Tuffley. GL4 23
Ribble Clo. GL3 26
Richmond Av. GL4 19
Richmond Gdns. GL2 16
Ridgemount Clo. GL3 21
Rissington Rd. GL4 23
Rivermead. GL2 14
Rivermead Clo. GL2 14
Riversley Rd. GL2 19
Robert Raikes Av. GL4 23
Roberts Rd. GL3 16
Robinhood St. GL1 18
Robins End. GL3 16
Robinson Rd. GL1 18
Robinswood Gdns. GL4 24
Rockleigh Clo. GL4 23
Rodney Clo. GL2 15
Roman Rd. GL4 20
Romney Clo. GL1 23
Rookery Rd. GL3 16
Rosebery Av. GL1 18
Rosemary Clo. GL4 24
Rowan Gdns. GL3 2
Royal Oak Rd. GL1 13
Rumsey Clo. GL4 25
Ruspidge Clo. GL4 25
Russell St. GL1 1
Russet Clo. GL4 2
Rustic Clo. GL4 24
Rydal Rd. GL2 15
Ryder Row. GL3 1
Ryecroft St. GL1 1
Ryelands. GL4 2

Saddlers Rd. GL2
Saffron Clo. GL4
Sage Clo. GL3
St Albans Rd. GL2
St Aldate St. GL1 1
St Aldwyn Rd. GL1
St Ann Way. GL1 1
St Annes Clo. GL3 2
St Barnabas Clo. GL1 2
St Catherine St. GL1 1
St Davids Clo. GL4 2
St Georges Clo. GL4 2
St Georges Rd. GL3 2
St James. GL2 2
St James Clo. GL2 2
St James St. GL1 1
St Johns Av. GL3 1
St Johns La. GL1 1
St Kilda Par. GL1 1
St Lawrence Rd. GL4 2
St Leonards Clo. GL4 2
St Lukes St. GL1 1
St Margarets Rd. GL3 2
St Mark St. GL1 1
St Mary St. GL1 1
St Marys Clo. GL1 1
St Marys Sq. GL1 1
St Michaels Sq. GL1 1
St Nicholas Sq. GL1 1
St Oswalds Rd. GL1 1
St Oswalds Trading Est. GL1
St Pauls Ct. GL1 1
St Pauls Rd. GL1 1
St Peters Rd. GL4 1
St Phillips Clo. GL3 1
St Swithuns Rd. GL2 1
St Vincents Way. GL3 1
Saintbridge Clo. GL4 1
Saintbridge Pl. GL4 1
Salisbury Rd. GL1 1
Salvia Clo. GL3
Sandalwood Dri. GL4
Sandfield Rd. GL3
Sandford Way. GL4
Sandhurst La. GL2
Sandhurst Rd. GL1
Sandown Lawn. GL3
Sandpiper Clo. GL2

dringham Av. GL4	23 E4
dstar Clo. GL2	16 A4
dycroft Rd. GL3	16 D2
dyleaze. GL2	19 H1
perton Rd. GL4	19 E6
phire Clo. GL4	23 E1
urn Clo. GL4	20 C5
ernake Rd. GL4	19 F4
on Clo. GL2	15 H4
Little Mews. GL2	16 B4
ers Cres. GL3	26 B2
ool La. GL2	22 A6
tt Av. GL2	23 E1
broke Rd. GL1	15 E6
brook Rd. GL3	26 B2
ert St. GL1	15 E6
ond Av. GL4	23 F3
gley Clo. GL4	23 E4
wyn Rd. GL4	23 H1
o Rd. GL1	14 D6
enth Av. GL4	23 F3
ern Oaks. GL2	22 B6
ern Rd. GL1	13 A4
erndale Dri. GL2	22 A5
mour Rd. GL1	18 C5
ckleton Clo. GL3	17 E4
kespeare Av. GL2	23 E2
mrock Clo. GL3	16 C3
arwater Gro. GL3	16 A3
ron Clo. GL2	16 A4
lley Av. GL2	23 E1
pherd Rd. GL2	22 D2
pherds Way. GL3	16 C2
rborne St. GL1	15 E6
rwood Grn. GL2	15 E3
rdington Rd. GL3	26 C2
ney St. GL1	19 F3
ock Clo. GL3	16 C2
er Birch Clo. GL2	22 B4
er Clo. GL4	23 E3
erdale Par. GL3	20 C3
mons Rd. GL2	20 C5
on Rd. GL2	15 G4
s La. GL2	22 C2
pe St. GL1	19 E3
on End. GL2	19 H1
on Rd. GL2	19 H1
ll Clo. GL2	15 F3
Acres. GL4	25 E3
ner St. GL1	13 E1
ark Way. GL4	19 G6
ey St. GL1	19 E4
bridge Rd. GL2	23 F3
edhams Rd. GL4	24 B4
wdon Gdns. GL3	16 D2
wdrop Clo. GL4	20 B6
wshill Clo. GL4	20 B4
iers Walk. GL3	21 E1
erset Pl. GL1	18 C3
el Clo. GL4	24 A1
th Clo. GL2	15 G5
thbrook Rd. GL4	19 H3
thern Av. GL4	23 G2
thfield Rd. GL4	23 G1
thgate St. GL1	13 B4
Rd. GL1	18 C3
tan Clo. GL4	20 B5
edwell Clo. GL4	20 B6
ncer Clo. GL3	20 C4
naker Rd. GL2	18 B3
ney Rd. GL4	20 B4
e Way. GL4	20 A3
ead Eagle Rd. GL1	13 E2
ngfield. GL2	22 B6
ngwell Gdns. GL3	17 E2
rrel Clo. GL2	22 B6
es Orchard. GL4	25 E2

Stamps Meadow. GL2	15 E4
Stank La. GL2	26 A4
Stanley Rd. GL1	18 D5
Stanley Ter. GL1	18 D5
Stanley Walk. GL4	25 F4
Stanmoor. GL4	24 D3
Stansby Cres. GL3	16 D3
Stanway Rd. GL4	19 H4
Station App. GL1	13 F3
Station Clo. GL3	17 F4
Station Rd. GL3	17 F5
Station Rd. GL1	13 E3
Staunton Clo. GL4	25 E1
Steeple Clo. GL4	20 A4
Stevan Clo. GL2	15 F4
Stewarts Mill La. GL4	25 E1
Sticky La. GL2	26 B3
Stirling Way. GL4	22 D3
Stone Clo. GL4	20 B4
Stonechat Av. GL4	19 H6
Stonehenge Rd. GL4	19 F4
Stowell Mws. GL4	20 A4
Stratford Clo. GL2	23 E1
Stratton Rd. GL1	19 E3
Stroud Rd. GL1	18 C3
Stroud Rd. GL4	23 G5
Sudbrook Way. GL4	19 G6
Sudgrove Clo. GL4	25 E1
Sudgrove Park. GL4	25 E1
Sudmeadow Rd. GL2	18 A2
Sulgrave Clo. GL4	23 E4
Summerland Dri. GL3	17 F4
Sunderland Ct. GL3	16 C2
Sunnycroft Mews. GL1	23 G1
Sunnyfield Rd. GL2	22 A6
Sussex Gdns. GL3	21 E4
Swallow Cres. GL3	16 A3
Swan Ct. GL1	13 B2
Swan Rd. GL1	15 E6
Sweetbriar St. GL1	15 E6
Swift Rd. GL4	20 A6
Swordfish Clo. GL3	17 E4
Sybil Rd. GL1	19 E5
Sycamore Clo. GL1	23 F1
Sydenham Ter. GL1	18 D5
Tainmor Clo. GL2	16 B4
Talbot Mews. GL1	18 C6
Tall Elms Clo. GL3	16 D4
Tallis Rd. GL3	16 C1
Tamar Rd. GL3	26 C2
Tandey Walk. GL3	16 B3
Tanners Clo. GL3	26 B1
Tarlton Clo. GL4	25 E2
Tarrington Rd. GL1	19 E5
Taurus Clo. GL2	15 E4
Taylors Ground. GL2	22 B4
Teal Clo. GL2	22 A4
Teddington Gdns. GL4	19 G6
Temple Clo. GL4	20 B3
Tennyson Av. GL2	23 E1
Tern Clo. GL4	20 A5
Tetbury Rd. GL4	23 G4
Tewkesbury Rd. GL2	15 E4
The Ash Path. GL4	25 E3
The Avenue. GL3	17 F4
The Avenue. GL2	15 H5
The Butts. GL4	24 A1
The Causeway. GL2	22 A4
The Chase. GL4	20 A6
The Chestnuts. GL1	18 C3
The Conifers. GL1	19 F4
The Copse. GL4	20 B4
The Crescent. GL3	21 G5
The Dawes. GL2	22 C5
The Dell. GL4	20 B4
The Dukeries. GL1	13 B2
The Firs. GL1	15 E6

The Forum. GL1	13 D4
The Furze. GL4	24 A1
The Hedgerow. GL2	15 G5
The Holly Grove. GL2	22 B6
The Holt. GL4	20 B4
The Lampreys. GL4	19 G5
The Laurels. GL1	19 E4
The Lawns. GL4	24 D3
The Lime. GL4	20 B4
The Malverns. GL4	20 A6
The Manor. GL3	17 E5
The Maples. GL4	20 B5
The Moat. GL2	22 B5
The Noake. GL3	21 E3
The Oaks. GL4	20 B4
The Orangery. GL4	20 B4
The Oval. GL1	18 C6
The Oxebode. GL1	13 D3
The Paddock. GL2	18 A5
The Piece. GL3	17 F5
The Plocks. GL3	17 F4
The Quay. GL1	13 A2
The Richmonds. GL4	24 D2
The Rudge. GL2	14 A1
The Stanley. GL4	25 F4
The Triangle. GL2	15 H6
The Tulworths. GL2	15 G4
The Vines. GL3	20 D4
The Wayridge. GL4	24 D2
The Wheatridge. GL4	24 C1
The Willows. GL2	22 B4
Theresa St. GL1	18 C4
Theyer Clo. GL3	26 B2
Thomas Moore Clo. GL3	16 D1
Thomas Stock Gdns. GL4	20 B5
Thomas St. GL1	19 E3
Thompson Way. GL3	16 A3
Thoresby Av. GL4	23 E5
Thornhill Clo. GL1	18 C6
Three Cocks La. GL1	13 C2
Thrush Clo. GL4	20 A5
Thyme Clo GL4	20 C6
Tidswell Clo. GL2	22 B6
Timmis Clo. GL4	24 C1
Tintern Rd. GL4	23 F2
Tirley Clo. GL2	22 A5
Tone Dri. GL3	26 C2
Towe Clo. GL4	20 A4
Trafalgar Dri. GL3	16 C1
Trajan Clo. GL4	20 D5
Tredworth Rd. GL1	19 E4
Trent Rd. GL3	26 C2
Trevor Rd. GL3	20 C5
Tribune Pl. GL4	20 B5
Trier Way. GL1	18 C3
Trubshaw Ct. GL3	17 E4
Tudor St. GL1	18 C5
Tuffley Av. GL1	18 B5
Tuffley Cres. GL1	18 C6
Tuffley La. GL4	22 D3
Tweenbrook Av. GL1	18 B5
Twyver Bank. GL4	25 F3
Twyver Clo. GL4	25 F3
Tyndale Rd. GL3	20 D4
Tynings Ct. GL3	17 F4
Ullenwood Rd. GL4	20 A4
Underhill Rd. GL4	24 C2
Union St. GL1	13 E1
Upper Quay St. GL1	13 B2
Upton Clo. GL3	20 B4
Upton Hill. GL4	24 D6
Upton La. GL4	25 E1
Upton St. GL1	19 F4
Usk Way. GL3	26 C2
Valerian Clo. GL4	20 B5
Valley La. GL4	25 G5

Vauxhall Rd. GL1	19 E3
Vauxhall Ter. GL1	19 E3
Vensfield Rd. GL2	22 B4
Verbena Clo. GL4	20 B6
Verburn Clo. GL4	25 F1
Vernal Clo. GL4	20 C6
Vertican Rd. GL3	16 A3
Vetch Clo. GL4	24 B1
Viburnum View. GL4	25 F1
Vicarage Clo. GL3	17 F5
Vicarage La. GL3	26 B1
Vicarage Rd. GL1	19 F4
Victoria Rd. GL2	15 E3
Victoria St. GL1	19 E3
Victory Clo. GL3	16 C2
Victory Rd. GL1	19 E5
Vincent Av. GL4	23 E5
Vine Ter. GL1	15 E6
Voyce Clo. GL4	23 F3
Vulcan Way. GL4	20 C5
Walham La. GL2	14 D5
Walnut Clo. GL4	24 D2
Walton Clo. GL4	25 E3
Ward Av. GL3	16 B3
Warren Clo. GL3	16 D2
Warwick Av. GL4	23 E4
Water Wheel Clo. GL4	22 A5
Watermans Ct. GL2	22 A5
Watermeadow. GL2	22 B6
Watermoor Ct. GL3	16 D4
Waters Reach. GL2	18 A5
Watery La. GL2	25 F5
Watson Gro. GL4	25 F1
Watts Clo. GL3	20 D5
Waverley Rd. GL2	19 G1
Weald Clo. GL4	24 C1
Weavers Rd. GL2	22 B4
Wedgwood Dri. GL2	15 H5
Weir Bridge Clo. GL4	20 B3
Well Cross Rd. GL4	24 A1
Wellesley St. GL1	19 E5
Wellington Par. GL1	13 F2
Wellington St. GL1	18 D3
Wells Rd. GL4	19 H3
Wellsprings Rd. GL2	15 G6
Welveland La. GL4	20 B3
Wentworth Clo. GL2	15 G4
West End La. GL3	21 E5
West End Par. GL1	14 B6
West End Ter. GL1	14 B6
West Lodge Dri. GL4	20 A5
Westbourne Dri. GL2	22 A6
Westbury Rd. GL4	23 F2
Westcote Rd. GL4	23 G4
Westfield Av. GL3	21 F5
Westfield Rd. GL3	21 F5
Westfield Ter. GL2	14 D4
Westgate St. GL1	13 A1
Westland Rd. GL2	26 B3
Wesley Ct. GL1	19 E3
Westmead Rd. GL2	16 A4
Weston Rd. GL1	18 D3
Westover Ct. GL3	16 D2
Whaddon Way. GL4	23 F5
Wheatridge Ct. GL4	24 D1
Wheatstone Rd. GL1	19 E5
Wheatway. GL4	24 D2
Whitebeam Clo. GL2	15 G4
Whiteway Rd. GL4	24 B1
Whitewell Clo. GL4	20 B3
Whitfield St. GL1	13 E3
Whittle Av. GL4	23 F4
Whornes Orchard. GL4	25 E3
Widden St. GL1	19 E3
Wigmore Clo. GL4	20 B6
Wilkes Av. GL3	20 D3
Willow Av. GL4	19 G4

Willow Croft Clo. GL4	24 D3
Willow Way. GL4	19 G5
Willowleaze. GL2	16 A6
Wilton Clo. GL1	18 C5
Wilton Rd. GL1	18 C6
Winchcombe Rd. GL4	23 G4
Winchester Dri. GL4	23 G3
Windermere Rd. GL2	15 H5
Windmill Cotts. GL1	19 F3
Windrush Rd. GL4	23 G4
Windsor Dri. GL4	23 E4
Winnycroft La. GL4	24 C5
Winsley Rd. GL4	24 C2
Winslow Pl. GL3	17 E3
Winston Rd. GL3	17 E4
Wishford Clo. GL2	16 B5
Witcomb Clo. GL4	25 E3
Withy Mews. GL4	19 G6
Woburn Av. GL4	23 E4
Wolseley Rd. GL2	19 G1
Woodbine Clo. GL4	20 B6
Woodcock Clo. GL4	20 A6
Woodcote. GL2	15 G4
Woodend Clo. GL4	20 B3
Woodford Clo. GL4	19 F5
Woodgate Clo. GL4	20 B4
Woodland Grn. GL4	25 E3
Woodpecker Rd. GL2	25 E1
Woodrow Way. GL2	22 D2
Woodruff Clo. GL4	24 B1
Woods Orchard. GL4	23 G4
Woods Orchard Rd. GL4	23 G4
Woolstrop Way. GL2	22 C2
Worcester Par. GL1	13 E1
Worcester St. GL1	13 E2
Wotton Ct. GL4	20 A2
Wotton Hill. GL2	19 F1
Wren Clo. GL4	19 G6
Wren Ter. GL3	16 A3
Wye Rd. GL3	26 C2
Yarrow Clo. GL4	24 A1
Yew Tree Way. GL3	16 D4
York Rd. GL4	19 H3
Zinnia Clo. GL3	16 C2
Zoons Rd. GL3	20 D3

SHURDINGTON

Badgeworth La. GL51	28 A2
Bishop Rd. GL51	28 B1
Blenheim Orchard. GL51	28 C1
Church La. GL51	28 B1
Cowls Mead. GL51	28 B1
Farm La. GL51	28 B2
Greenway Clo. GL51	28 B2
Greenway La. GL51	28 B2
Gwinnett Ct. GL51	28 C1
Harrison Rd. GL51	28 B2
Lambert Av. GL51	28 A2
Lambert Clo. GL51	28 B2
Lambert Dri. GL51	28 B2
Lambert Gdns. GL51	28 B2
Lambert Ter. GL51	28 B2
Laurence Clo. GL51	28 B1
Lawn Cres. GL51	28 C1
Leckhampton La. GL51	28 C1
Robertson Rd. GL51	28 B1
School La. GL51	28 C1
Shurdington Rd. GL51	28 B2
Sinclair Rd. GL51	28 B2
The Orchard Gro. GL51	28 B2
Vicarage Clo. GL51	28 C1
Wilson Rd. GL51	28 B2
Yarnolds. GL51	28 B2

ESTATE PUBLICATIONS

STREET ATLASES

ALFRETON, BELPER, RIPLEY
ASHFORD, TENTERDEN
BANGOR, CAERNARFON
BARNSTAPLE, ILFRACOMBE
BASILDON, BILLERICAY
BASINGSTOKE, ANDOVER
BATH, BRADFORD-ON-AVON
BEDFORD
BOURNEMOUTH, POOLE, CHRISTCHURCH
BRENTWOOD
BRIGHTON, LEWES, NEWHAVEN, SEAFORD
BRISTOL
BROMLEY (London Borough)
BURTON-ON-TRENT
BURY ST. EDMUNDS
CAMBRIDGE
CARDIFF
CHELMSFORD, BRAINTREE, MALDON, WITHAM
CHESTER
CHESTERFIELD
CHICHESTER, BOGNOR REGIS
COATBRIDGE, AIRDRIE
COLCHESTER, CLACTON
CONNAH'S QUAY
CORBY, KETTERING
CRAWLEY & MID SUSSEX
CREWE
DERBY, HEANOR, CASTLE DONINGTON
EASTBOURNE
EDINBURGH, MUSSELBURGH
EXETER, EXMOUTH
FALKIRK, GRANGEMOUTH
FAREHAM, GOSPORT
FOLKESTONE, DOVER, DEAL
GLASGOW & PAISLEY
GLOUCESTER, CHELTENHAM
GRAVESEND, DARTFORD
GRAYS, THURROCK
GRIMSBY, CLEETHORPES
GUILDFORD, WOKING
HAMILTON, MOTHERWELL
HARLOW, BISHOPS STORTFORD
HASTINGS
HERTFORD, HODDESDON
HIGH WYCOMBE
HUNTINGDON, ST. NEOTS
IPSWICH, FELIXSTOWE
ISLE OF WIGHT TOWNS
KINGSTON-UPON-HULL
LANCASTER, MORECAMBE
LEICESTER, LOUGHBOROUGH
LINCOLN
LLANDUDNO, COLWYN BAY
LUTON, DUNSTABLE
MAIDSTONE
MANSFIELD
MEDWAY, GILLINGHAM
MILTON KEYNES
NEW FOREST TOWNS
NEWPORT, CHEPSTOW
NEWTOWN, WELSHPOOL
NORTHAMPTON
NORWICH
NOTTINGHAM, EASTWOOD, HUCKNALL, ILKESTON
OXFORD, ABINGDON
PETERBOROUGH
PLYMOUTH, IVYBRIDGE, SALTASH, TORPOINT
PORTSMOUTH, HAVANT
READING
REIGATE, BANSTEAD, LEATHERHEAD, DORKING
RHYL, PRESTATYN
ST. ALBANS, WELWYN, HATFIELD
SALISBURY, AMESBURY, WILTON
SCUNTHORPE
SEVENOAKS
SHREWSBURY
SITTINGBOURNE, FAVERSHAM
SLOUGH, MAIDENHEAD
SOUTHAMPTON, EASTLEIGH

SOUTHEND-ON-SEA
STAFFORD
STEVENAGE, HITCHIN
STIRLING
STOKE ON TRENT
STROUD, NAILSWORTH
SWANSEA, NEATH
SWINDON, CHIPPENHAM
TAUNTON, BRIDGWATER
TELFORD
THANET, CANTERBURY, HERNE BAY, WHITSTABLE
TORBAY
TRURO & FALMOUTH
TUNBRIDGE WELLS, TONBRIDGE, CROWBOROUGH
WATFORD, HEMEL HEMPSTEAD
WEALDEN TOWNS
WELLINGBOROUGH
WESTON-SUPER-MARE
WEYMOUTH, DORCHESTER
WINCHESTER, NEW ALRESFORD
WORTHING, LITTLEHAMPTON, ARUNDEL
WREXHAM

LEISURE MAPS

SOUTH EAST ENGLAND (1:200,000)
KENT & EAST SUSSEX (1:150,000)
SUSSEX & SURREY (1:150,000
SOUTHERN ENGLAND (1:200,000)
ISLE OF WIGHT (1:50,000)
WESSEX (1:200,000)
DEVON & CORNWALL (1:200,000)
CORNWALL (1:180,000)
DEVON (1:200,000)
DARTMOOR & SOUTH DEVON COAST (1:100,000)
EXMOOR & NORTH DEVON COAST (1:100,000)
GREATER LONDON M25 (1:80,000)
EAST ANGLIA (1:200,000)
CHILTERNS & THAMES VALLEY (1:200,000)
THE COTSWOLDS (1:110,000)
COTSWOLDS & WYEDEAN (1:200,000)
WALES (1:250,000)
CYMRU (1;250,000)
THE SHIRES OF MIDDLE ENGLAND (1:250,000)
STAFFORDSHIRE & SHROPSHIRE (1:200,000)
PEAK DISTRICT (1:100,000)
SNOWDONIA (1:125,000)
YORKSHIRE (1:200,000)
YORKSHIRE DALES (1:125,000)
NORTH YORKSHIRE MOORS (1:125,000)
NORTH WEST ENGLAND (1:200,000)
ISLE OF MAN (1:60,000)
NORTH PENNINES & LAKES (1:200,000)
LAKE DISTRICT (1:75,000)
BORDERS OF ENGLAND & SCOTLAND (1:200,000)
BURNS COUNTRY (1:200,000)
HEART OF SCOTLAND (1:200,000)
GREATER GLASGOW (1:150,000)
EDINBURGH & THE LOTHIANS (1:150,000)
ISLE OF ARRAN (1:63,360)
FIFE (1:100,000)
LOCH LOMOND & TROSSACHS (1:150,000)
ARGYLL & LOCH LOMOND (1:275,000)
PERTHSHIRE (1:150,000)
FORT WILLIAM, BEN NEVIS, GLEN COE (1:185,000)
IONA (1:10,000) & MULL (1:115,000)
GRAMPIAN HIGHLANDS (1:185,000)
LOCH NESS & INVERNESS (1:150,000)
AVIEMORE & SPEY VALLEY (1:150,000)
SKYE & LOCHALSH (1:130,000)
ARGYLL & THE ISLES (1:200,000)
CAITHNESS & SUTHERLAND (1:185,000)
HIGHLANDS OF SCOTLAND (1:275,000)
WESTERN ISLES (1:125,000)
ORKNEY & SHETLAND (1:128,000)
ENGLAND & WALES (1:650,000)
SCOTLAND (1:500,000)
HISTORIC SCOTLAND (1:500,000)
SCOTLAND CLAN MAP (1:625,000)
BRITISH ISLES (1:1,100,000)
GREAT BRITAIN (1:1,100,000)

COUNTY ATLASES

BEDFORDSHIRE
BERKSHIRE
BUCKINGHAMSHIRE
CAMBRIDGESHIRE
CHESHIRE
CORNWALL
DERBYSHIRE
DEVON
DORSET
ESSEX
GLOUCESTERSHIRE
HAMPSHIRE
HERTFORDSHIRE
KENT
LEICESTERSHIRE
NORTHAMPTONSHIRE
NOTTINGHAMSHIRE

OXFORDSHIRE
SHROPSHIRE
SOMERSET
STAFFORDSHIRE
SURREY
SUSSEX (EAST)
SUSSEX (WEST)
WILTSHIRE

OTHER MAPS

KENT TO CORNWALL (1:460,000)
COUNTY MAP — DORSET
— HAMPSHIRE
— SOMERSET
— WILTSHIRE
SOUTH EAST ASIA (1:6,000,000)
CHINA (1:6,000,000)
NEPAL (1;800,000)

STREET PLANS

BODMIN & WADEBRIDGE
CAMBORNE & REDRUTH
EDINBURGH TOURIST PLAN
NEWQUAY
PENZANCE & ST. IVES
ST. ALBANS
ST. AUSTELL

EUROPEAN LEISURE MAPS

EUROPE (1:3,100,000)
BENELUX (1:600,000)
FRANCE (1:1,000,000)
GERMANY (1:1,000,000)
IRELAND (1:625,000)
ITALY (1:1,000,000)

SCANDINAVIA (1:2,600,000)
SPAIN & PORTUGAL (1:100,000)
CROSS CHANNEL VISITORS' MAP (1:530,0
WORLD (1:35,000,000)
WORLD FLAT

NORTH FRENCH TOWNS ATLAS
BOULOGNE SHOPPERS MAP
CALAIS SHOPPERS MAP
DIEPPE SHOPPERS MAP

ESTATE PUBLICATIONS are also
Distributors in the U.K. for:
INTERNATIONAL TRAVEL MAPS, Canada

Catalogue and prices from ESTATE PUBLICATIONS,
Bridewell House, Tenterden, Kent. TN30 6EP.
Tel: 01580 764225   Fax: 01580 763720